The Quilter's Palette

The Quilter's Palette

A Workbook of Color
& Pattern Ideas
& Effects

KATY DENNY

Creative Publishing
international

First published in the United States of America by
Creative Publishing international, Inc., a member of
Quayside Publishing Group
400 First Avenue North
Suite 400
Minneapolis, MN 55401
1-800-328-3895
www.creativepub.com
Visit www.Craftside.Typepad.com for a behind-the-scenes peek at our crafty world!

Conceived, designed, and produced by
Quid Publishing
Level 4, Sheridan House
114 Western Road
Hove BN3 1DD
England

ISBN: 978-1-58923-799-5

10 9 8 7 6 5 4 3 2 1

Printed in China

For Anthony, Kate, Lin, and Elizabeth, whose invaluable help
and support made this book possible

Contents

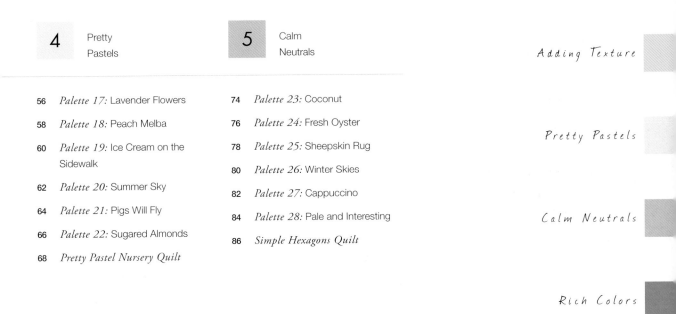

Understanding Color

Understanding Pattern

Adding Texture

Pretty Pastels

Calm Neutrals

Rich Colors

Cool Hues

Warm Tones

Clear Contrasts

Putting It All Together

Introduction

The range of fabrics available for patchwork and quilting is gigantic, which is both wonderful and a little overwhelming. New ranges come in and out of the fabric stores so frequently now that by the time you've picked out a quilt pattern to follow you often have to make fabric substitutions—the ones in the pattern are no longer available, or are out of stock. Although this is a great opportunity to add your own stamp to your quilts, making decisions about which fabrics to combine and with which quilt block patterns can be daunting.

The first three chapters of this book will help you to understand how colors, patterns, and textures work together to create different effects. You may have come across much of the information before, either at school in art class or through your own creative explorations. What I hope I've done here is to make color theory, ideas about pattern, and the nature of texture relevant to patchwork and quilting specifically.

Chapters 4–9 each have a color theme and contain various fabric and block combinations that explore aspects of the theme. You'll find an eclectic mix of classic and modern, subtle and eye-popping choices that should help you to see the range of effects possible. Each palette within these chapters has three block pattern examples, so you can see that even within a certain combination of fabric choices, the block pattern you select can really change the way the fabrics work together.

Of course, it's all very well seeing fabrics combined in individual quilt blocks, but what will they look like in a whole quilt, together with the binding and any textural pattern that the quilting adds? At the end of each of Chapters 2–9 you'll find a finished quilt to illustrate one of the fabric palettes from that chapter. Each quilt has step-by-step instructions, a diagram to show how the blocks fit together, and a photograph to show the quilt "in situ."

Linda Clements, a technical genius when it comes to quilting, has put together the assembly instructions and diagrams in Chapter 10, the final part of the book. Here you will find all the technical information you need to make each of the 50 quilt block patterns used throughout the book's 52 different fabric palettes, as well as instructions on how to construct and bind a basic quilt.

I've been playing with pattern and color in all sorts of ways since I was little, and although a relative newcomer to quilting, I've been sewing (and collecting fabrics) for many years. The feeling when you put certain colors and patterns together and the whole combination becomes more than the sum of its parts is what drives me creatively, and I hope that with this book I can not only share color, pattern, and block combinations to inspire you, but also enable you to gain the confidence to make your own decisions about what goes well together for your own quilt designs and fabric combinations. Have fun!

Katy Denny

1 Understanding Color

If you don't feel confident making color choices for your quilts, read on! Once you've found a fabric that you love it can be difficult to decide what to put with it that will look "right." You can cut down on the time spent experimenting by understanding a little more about how different colors work with each other for different effects.

If you're in a "color rut," this chapter will help you to understand how to branch out a little. I found myself with a range of green and pink fabrics and not much else a few years ago, and though these colors still feature strongly in my stash, I now also have plenty of purple, turquoise, and yellow to ring the changes. I'm not suggesting that everyone has to use every color of the rainbow, but it can be refreshing to introduce touches of new colors here and there, if only to breathe new life into your old favorites.

Every color can look brighter or more subdued depending on which other color or colors it is combined with, and this can have a huge impact on the overall visual effect of a quilt. By the end of this chapter you'll be able to combine colors with ease to give the effect that you want, whether it's a fresh, spring-themed child's quilt or a sophisticated, tonal quilt in calming neutral shades.

What is Color?

Color is our perception of reflected or refracted light. Special parts of our eyes, the rods and cones, have receptors that detect different frequencies of light, and it is these variations in frequency that translate into colors when our brains process the signals from our eyes. As a consequence, everyone perceives color slightly differently.

The Color Wheel

The color wheel is the most common way to show the relationships between different colors. As most of us learned at school, all colors are made from combinations of the three primary colors: yellow, blue, and red. Secondary colors are those made from equal amounts of two primaries: Yellow and blue make green; yellow and red make orange; red and blue make purple. If you mix a primary (say, red) with its neighboring secondary (orange), you get a tertiary color: red-orange.

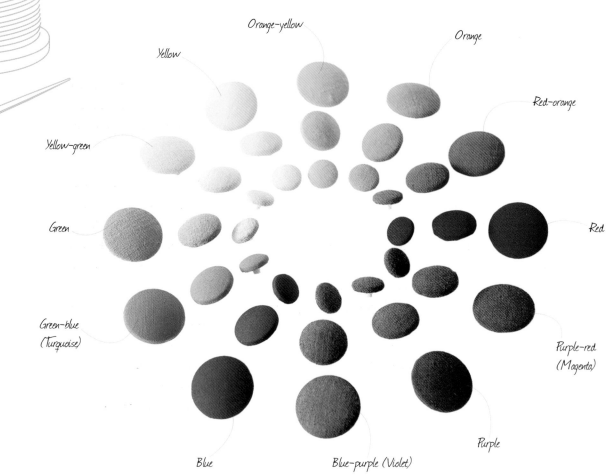

Orange-yellow

Yellow

Orange

Red-orange

Yellow-green

Green

Red

Green-blue
(Turquoise)

Purple-red
(Magenta)

Purple

Blue

Blue-purple (Violet)

Philip Jacobs has used plenty of rich colors in his Japanese Chrysanthemum design, but the balance of warm plum with cool violet and warm yellow-green with cool blue-green allows the pattern of the chrysanthemum flowers and foliage to remain distinct.

Warm and Cool Colors

The colors on the red side of the color wheel are usually thought of as the "warm" colors, whereas those on the blue side of the wheel are the "cool" colors. The colors in-between can go either way—for example, purple can be warm or cool depending on the exact proportions of red and blue used to make the color.

Balancing warm and cool colors is a great way of achieving a contrasting yet harmonious design. If you're having trouble making your fabric choices work together, bear in mind that changing your shade of green, for example, from a warm yellow-green to a cool blue-green can make all the difference.

Tone

If colors are the same tone, they are the same "lightness" or "darkness," and if you photocopied them side by side in black and white, the resultant photocopy would be all the same shade of gray. This sounds simple, but it can be hard to judge tone with different colors because of the other elements that come into play, such as whether they are warm or cool colors.

Being aware of the tonal values of your fabric choices can help you to create the effects you want—more difference between the tones for a contrasting, bold effect, or similar tones for a subtler creation.

Tints, Shades, and Tones

In addition to the three primary colors of red, blue, and yellow, we also need black and white in order to create the vast array of tints, shades, and tones of each of the primary, secondary, and tertiary hues. Black and white are not technically colors at all, but the absence of color (black) or full saturation of all the primaries (white). In practical terms, when creating patterned or colored fabric, black is a physical dye, and white is usually the absence of any dye, allowing the white of the cloth to come through into the pattern.

❖ **Tints:** these are pure colors with varying degrees of white added to create pastel colors such as those in palettes 18 and 22.

❖ **Shades:** these are pure colors with varying degrees of black added, to create deep, rich colors such as those in palettes 41 and 46.

❖ **Tones:** these are pure colors where both black and white have been added in varying degrees, to give more subtle versions of a color. See palette 36 for an example of tones being used without any stronger colors in the mix.

If you look at some of the more complex fabric patterns in this book, or even better, take a look in your local fabric store, you'll see that designers tend to use a combination of pure colors with their tints, shades, or tones to make patterns that are complex yet pleasing to the eye. See the Chinese patterned fabrics in palette 41, or the patterned fabrics by Kaffe Fassett in palette 34—look closely and you may be surprised at the number of different colors and shades, tones and tints you can spot!

Color Relationships

Neighboring colors on the color wheel are called analogous colors. So if you chose yellow, yellow-green, and green for your quilt fabrics, you would have an analogous color scheme. These combinations tend to be harmonious and easy on the eye, with the colors blending together—look at the quilt on page 122 to see for yourself.

Opposite colors on the color wheel are called complementary colors. So if you chose green and magenta for your quilt fabrics, you would have a complementary color scheme. Unlike analogous schemes, complementary ones are bright and vibrant—see the quilt on page 104 as an example.

In between analogous and complementary color schemes is a whole host of different possibilities that will give different effects.

Color Balance

Most fabric designs—and most quilt designs—are more complex than the analogous or complementary palettes on pages 17 and 18. And finding a balance between light and dark, warm and cool, bright and subtle that's pleasing to your eye is where the real fun starts.

The great thing about patchwork and quilting is that the fabric designer has often done much of this work for you—if you choose a fabric you love that has a multitude of colors within its pattern, the simplest way to add more fabrics to your quilt palette is to hunt for those containing some of the same colors. You could choose more patterned fabrics from the same range, as designers always endeavor to put collections together that work harmoniously and share the same overall range of colors (even if not every fabric in the collection contains each color in the range).

Split Complementary and Triadic Schemes

If you want to include three main colors in your quilt palette, a good way to make sure they balance is to use either a split complementary or a triadic scheme. With a split complementary scheme, one color will be on one side of the wheel, and the other two will be almost opposite—in fact, one each side of the color directly opposite (see palette 4, page 19). For example, you could choose purple-red with yellow and green, or blue with red-orange and orange-yellow.

For a triadic color scheme, each of your choices should be equally spaced around the wheel (see palette 44, page 134). Green, purple, and orange are not only all the secondary colors, but also a triadic color scheme. Once you bring tints and shades of each of the colors into the mix you can attain more sophisticated palettes, not to mention adding in patterned fabrics where there will usually be not only a predominant color but others at play too. (For more on pattern see Chapter 2.)

Neutral Colors

Neutral colors are a quilter's best friend. They don't fight, clash, or argue with each other—they get along beautifully and don't mind sitting next to any color you throw at them. Gray, brown, and cream—and all their tints, shades, and tones—are technically "colors," but it's usually so hard to determine what their component hues are that they simply serve as a foil for brighter colors in a fabric pattern or quilt design. These neutrals can be used to great effect to balance or harmonize a design.

It's worth thinking carefully about tone when you decide which neutrals to add to a quilt palette. If you add a deep-toned neutral such as black to pale tints such as pastels, you will have a dramatic effect due to the tonal contrast (see the fabric patterns in palette 47, page 146). If your neutral is of a similar tone those of your colors, it acts as a foil for the colored fabrics, harmonizing their different patterns but not adding drama (see palette 19, page 60).

Neutrals can, of course, be used by themselves for soft, soothing designs. All the palettes in Chapter 5 use plenty of them (see pages 74–85). You'll see that the greater the tonal contrast, the clearer and cleaner the block designs, and that where a little color is included, it really stands out against such a subtle backdrop (see palette 26, page 80).

1 Shades of Gray

This palette is deliberately color-free, to demonstrate the effects that can be achieved with different tones. You can see how the textured fabric (4) immediately adds visual interest in contrast to the solids, though from a distance the effect is a solid mid-light gray.

Fabric Choices

1 Free Spirit Designer Solids, Manatee

2 Free Spirit Designer Solids, Slate Gray

3 Klona Cotton, Ash

4 Carolyn Friedlander Architextures Crosshatch, Gray

Log Cabin

This block is a great way to demonstrate how tone can be used to create visual effects. By using the two lightest fabrics on one side and the two darkest on the other side, the block has a sort of diagonal split. Imagine combining numerous blocks like this—you could create a really striking quilt. See page 184 for block-making instructions.

Palette

2 Analogous Blues

These fabrics have all been chosen because they sit together on the color wheel, creating an analogous color scheme. The patterned fabric introduces a little white, too, which adds a freshness to the scheme.

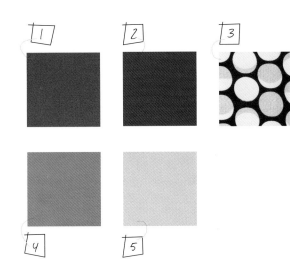

Fabric Choices

1. Klona Cotton, Dresden

2. Klona Cotton, Royal

3. Lizzy House Constellations Moonphase, Night

4. Free Spirit Designer Solids, Rocket Blue

5. Moda Bella Solids, Blue Raspberry

Friendship Star

In this version of the Friendship Star the choice of fabrics means that the star shape is quite subtle, and relies on the difference in tone between the star fabrics and the outer fabrics for definition. For block-making instructions see page 199.

3 Complementary Colors

Sitting on opposite sides of the color wheel, the complementary combination of blue and orange is a classic choice. Tonally the fabric choices are all very similar, but because of their opposing colors, the blues are very distinct from the oranges.

Fabric Choices

1 Kaffe Fassett Roman Glass, Blue

2 Anna Maria Horner Field Study
Fine Feathered Ghost, Pomegranate

3 Free Spirit Pinwheels, Orange

4 Liberty Lord Paisley, H

Friendship Star

The block pattern is much more distinct in this version of the Friendship Star due to the complementary colors in the fabric palette. Although the different patterns used complicate the lines of the actual block, the orange choices in the central star contrast so absolutely with the blues on the outer area that the effect is really striking. For block-making instructions see page 199.

Palette

4 Split Complementary Colors

This is a progression of palettes 2 and 3, and the same block has been used so that the three palettes can be directly compared. You can see that here the design has more color complexity yet still has the "wow" factor of the complementary scheme in palette 3.

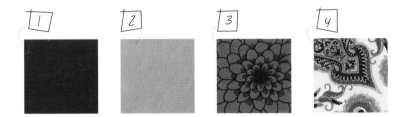

Fabric Choices

1 Kaffe Fassett Shot Cottons, Cobalt

2 Kaffe Fassett Shot Cottons, Sunshine

3 Kaffe Fassett Line Dance, Red

4 Liberty Lord Paisley, H

Friendship Star

The shape of the star is distinct against its background of blues but is more interesting to look at than the block in palette 3 as it contains a little color contrast with the red-orange and orange-yellow. For block-making instructions see page 199.

2 Understanding Pattern

Working with fabrics in all kinds of patterns is one of the things that makes patchwork and quilting such fun. But with all the fabric choices available it can be hard to decide which ones will look best together! Not only do you need to consider the patterns in the fabrics, you also have the quilt blocks bringing in their own layer of pattern to an overall quilt design.

How to navigate this complicated pattern maze? Break it down into the elements at work and you'll soon be confidently making great pattern choices that achieve the visual effects you desire. This chapter will help you to understand the different kinds of pattern, from soft florals and subtle textures to modern geometrics and bold stripes.

The fabric palettes in this chapter illustrate the effects you can achieve when combining pattern types, and what happens when you bring in different block patterns. The examples here should help you to visualize what your own choices will look like when sewn together in a quilt, avoiding frustrating results.

What is Pattern?

Pattern is all around us, from tree branches silhouetted against the sky to raindrops on a windowpane, from bricks in a wall to the ripples on a lake. And the number of patterns available in fabric form is colossal: spots, stripes, zigzags, florals, birds, spirals, webs, wax prints... all in a glorious array of colors, sizes, and complexities.

Combining Patterns

Putting patterned fabrics together to make a quilt can be one of the most rewarding—and frustrating—creative processes. New fabric ranges are usually launched with a variety of different patterns in a coordinating palette, which is a great way to ensure that your fabrics work together. But what if you want to combine fabrics from your stash with something new? Or what if your budget will only allow for a quarter of the new designer fabrics you love along with more classic patterns and colors? Anything is possible once you understand the different effects that can be achieved by using certain patterns together.

This Spring 2012 range from Tilda has lots of different patterns within it, but they are anchored in the fresh, simple palette of pinks and turquoises.

Both of these fabrics are designed by Amy Butler, and although their colors and styles go together perfectly, the pattern scales are very different. It's easy to see that the effect of the large flower pattern would be lost if only using a 2in square of fabric, whereas the small-scale pattern would retain the same look.

Pattern Scale

The scale of a pattern is easy to overlook, but it is, in fact, crucial when planning a quilt. Large-scale prints are fabulous for large-scale uses, but bear in mind that when only small amounts of fabric are needed for a quilt block, the pattern that you see on the fabric bolt can take on a very different character. Though a potential problem, this can also be used to advantage—for example, you can choose certain areas of the pattern that best suit your needs, allowing the individual sections to take on a new character of their own.

The cream background and black pattern outlines in "Summersville," by Lucie Summers, create a simple pattern of stylized shapes. By contrast, the classic Liberty print fabric uses three tones of pink to give flower petals a more realistic, albeit stylized, look.

Color and Pattern

Patterns in fabric are made up of different combinations of colors. These can be used to create realistic three-dimensional looking elements, such as flowers or animals. This will normally entail using lots of tints and shades of each color, and the fabric will have a complex palette. At the other end of the scale, colors can be used to create a more stylized effect of outlines or silhouettes, and this will typically involve far fewer shades. At its simplest, a pattern will involve just two colors—the background and the pattern. In general, the more complex the pattern, the more careful you need to be when combining it with other fabrics.

Fabric Patterns

Fabrics come in a huge range of patterns, and the choice can be overwhelming. By thinking of pattern in terms of type, as well as scale, it can be easier to determine what you are looking for to create a particular effect or to tie in with other fabrics from your stash.

It is usually easier to put patterns of the same type together successfully in a quilt than mixing lots of types. For example, mixing different florals together will usually create a harmonious palette, but mixing geometric patterns with florals and adding spots and textures could easily result in visual disaster.

But there is a happy medium, where two or three pattern types can be put together—it's just a case of making thoughtful choices. A geometric pattern with plenty of straight lines will almost always go well with stripes. Polka dots will usually look great with florals and their curvaceous lines. And if the color choices are restricted then most patterns can be combined, because the colors will make the palette come together.

Stripes

Stripes are one of the simplest forms of pattern and come in many styles, from straight, evenly spaced colored stripes to wiggly lines. They are extremely useful for adding visual interest to your fabric choices without fighting too much with other patterns. Because a stripe pattern is so simple, the color choices in the fabric play a huge part in how vibrant or subtle the overall effect is. A range of pure colors set against white, for example, will look really eye-catching, whereas softer colors or neutrals with cream or gray would have a much quieter presence.

Geometric Patterns

Moving on from stripes, geometric patterns have clear, distinct, simple shapes and often include triangles, circles, squares, and lines. They are usually a little more complex for the eye than stripes, but still have the ability to fit in with many other fabric types. If you're struggling to make geometrics look "right" with other fabric types, try mixing angular geometrics with other angular patterns (such as stripes or checks), and curvaceous geometrics with more rounded patterns such as florals or paisleys.

There is a vast range of striped fabrics available, and they make a great addition to any fabric stash.

Spots and Dots

Like stripes, spots and dots are so simple that they make great fabrics to combine with other patterns. Polka dots are regular, evenly spaced dots and come in a range of sizes and colorways. But other irregular spot or dot patterns can also look great either with plains or other patterns.

Dotty fabrics are available in a variety of colors, making them a great choice for blending in with other fabrics in a design.

Not all florals and paisleys go well together, but you can see from the sheer range that there are plenty of options for happy relationships.

Florals and Paisleys

From lifelike sprays of roses in soft pinks to stylized exotic blooms in bright block colors, floral fabrics come in many different styles. What they share is the curvaceous shapes of flowers and foliage, and, apart from some of the more modern damask-like designs, a natural feel. Paisley patterns—stylized Persian designs that contain intricate details within a twisted tear-shaped motif—also have a curvaceous, natural feel. Both pattern types combine well with other curvy patterns and with each other, so long as the fabric colors are either very similar or different enough to create a vibrant effect. Watch out for pattern styles—traditional florals do not always sit happily next to modern, more stylized designs. Similarly, scale has an impact on both florals and paisleys, and you're more likely to have a successful palette with similar-scale fabrics than by combining very large- and very small-scale patterns.

Patterns From Texture

When you are choosing fabrics for patchwork quilts, more often than not they will be light cottons with an even weave. If they have a pattern, it will be a design printed on top of the fabric with fabric dye or ink. However, there are many fabrics available that embody a pattern within the weave of the cloth, or have a specific texture that can bring an element of pattern when combined with contrasting textures. These kinds of fabrics—brocades, damasks, velvets, linens—tend to be heavier than the usual quilting cottons and can only be dry-cleaned, but there's no reason not to use them in a quilt so long as it isn't going to need frequent cleaning and your machine can cope with heavyweight fabrics.

Working with Heavyweight Fabrics

Although beautiful quilts can be made from heavier fabrics, they need to be constructed a little differently from those made from standard quilting cotton fabrics.

Just a small selection of fabrics that embody their pattern within their texture. From left to right, woolen tweed, cotton broderie anglaise, woven cotton damask.

❖ Ensure the fabrics you use in your quilt are all of a similar weight.

❖ Use a bigger seam allowance—½in or even larger, depending on how much the fabric is prone to fraying.

❖ Work with larger pieces of fabric and keep blocks simple. It's harder to make heavy fabric behave at corners or on curves.

❖ Use thick batting as your seams will be bulkier than usual.

❖ You may need to quilt by hand or send your quilt for professional long-arm quilting.

❖ Never put the quilt in the washing machine—have it professionally dry-cleaned if it gets grubby.

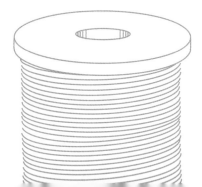

Patterns Within Quilt Blocks

The quilt blocks you decide to use in making a quilt add their own element of pattern, on top of those from fabrics and textures. Even the most basic block—a square or rectangle of fabric—will create a patterned effect once repeated across a quilt, because the seams between fabric pieces will form a lattice pattern, and the contrast in fabrics creates a patchwork pattern. This is further enhanced when more complex blocks are used, and a huge range of potential patterns and visual effects is therefore available.

Choosing Blocks

There are hundreds of quilt blocks to choose from. In this book 50 different blocks are used, and instructions on how to make each one can be found in Chapter 10. Some blocks are faster to piece than others, so if time is short and you want a finished quilt rather than a "work in progress," be sure to choose from the simpler blocks, or combine simple blocks with a small number of more complex ones.

Block Pattern vs Fabric Pattern

The pattern of a block when combined with the pattern within a fabric will create its own visual effect. It's important to think about how your fabrics will look once pieced in hexagons, triangles, stripes, or squares, as some block patterns will suit certain fabric patterns better than others, and vice versa.

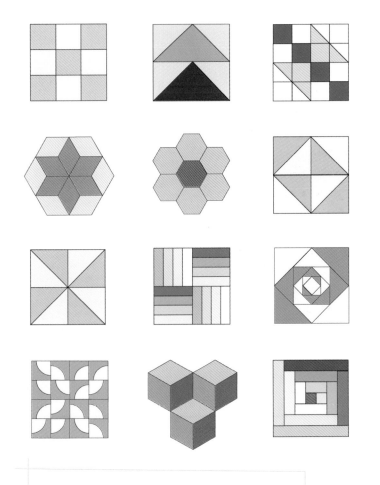

These thumbnail illustrations show 12 of the 50 blocks from this book. Even in this limited range you can see the many patterns that can be created by piecing fabric in different ways.

5 Triangles and Stripes

When your fabric choices include patterns with straight lines it's important to consider your block pattern carefully, and also to be watchful of your piecing. The line of a stripe at a definite angle to a block seam will look dynamic, whereas a line or stripe at a very slight angle to a seam could look messy.

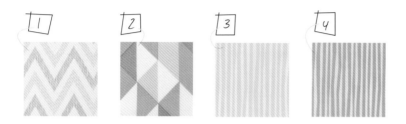

Fabric Choices

1 | Michelle Engel Bencsko Simpatico Chevrons, Golden

2 | Michelle Engel Bencsko Simpatico On Point, Peachy

3 | Michelle Engel Bencsko Simpatico Straws, Golden

4 | Michelle Engel Bencsko Simpatico Straws, Peachy

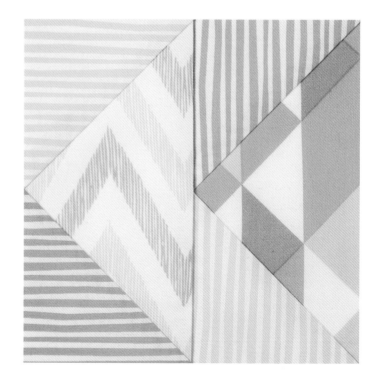

Flying Geese

This is a classic block pattern that enjoys perennial popularity. You can see how the triangles in the block echo the triangles in fabric 2, but aren't entirely comfortable with fabric 1. For block-making instructions see page 174.

Palette

6 Florals, Spots, and Paisleys

In this palette all of the fabrics are from the same range, and the
designer has combined florals, paisley, and polka dots to create a pretty
but modern range of fabric designs.

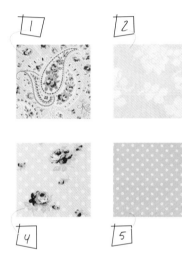

1
2
3
4
5

Fabric Choices

1 Tanya Whelan Delilah Paisley, Blue

2 Tanya Whelan Delilah Rosie, Blue

3 Tanya Whelan Delilah Dots, Blue

4 Tanya Whelan Delilah Buds, Blue

5 Tanya Whelan Delilah Dots, Green

Flying Geese

By using the polka dot fabrics in the
large triangles of the Flying Geese
and the paisley and floral patterns
in the smaller triangles, the look of
this block is modern and fun. By
repeating blocks like this at the same
orientation across a whole quilt you'd
have a vertical stripe effect created by
the dot fabrics. For block-making
instructions see page 174.

7 Textural Patterns

Although what we think of as quilting fabrics are plain, smooth cotton, there is no law to say you can't make quilts from any sort of fabric. The key is to ensure all of the fabrics you use are of a similar weight and only ever to dry-clean the finished quilt. This palette uses a combination of heavy Chinese brocade and heavy Italian wool drape fabric. Note the contrast between the matte plain wool and the shiny satin background of the brocades, and how not only color but also the woven texture of the brocades brings out their patterns.

Fabric Choices

1 Heavyweight woven wool cloth in beige

2 Deep blue Chinese brocade with dragon pattern

3 Mid-blue Chinese brocade with cherry blossom pattern

Flying Geese

The Flying Geese pattern helps to emphasize the textural pattern of the brocades by placing them against a plain, matte background. As the fabrics are heavy and prone to frayed edges the seam allowance used in this block is ½in rather than the usual ¼in. For block-making instructions see page 174.

8 Hexagons and Stripes

The angles within hexagon blocks can have a dramatic effect when used with striped fabrics. The colors in this palette have been chosen to reflect the Grandmother's Flower Garden block title, but the effect is about as far from floral as possible. While not to everyone's taste and potentially headache inducing, the riot of angular lines demonstrates the power of combining certain fabric patterns with certain block patterns. (See page 81 for a very different look for this block.)

Grandmother's Flower Garden

This block is simply pieced hexagons, but with careful choice of fabric color and tone a "flower" effect is produced. Here, the green stripes are acting as "foliage" with the other two fabrics creating the colored "flower"—though the stripes have been made so eye-popping when used in hexagon blocks that the flower isn't immediately obvious. For block-making instructions see page 206.

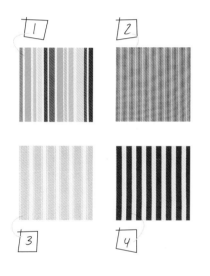

Fabric Choices

[1] Michael Miller Cocoa Berry That's All, Berry

[2] Maywood Studios American Beauty, 14

[3] Vintage sage green and white stripe cotton

[4] Red and white ¼in stripe cotton

9 Triangles and Florals

The block pattern here uses many Half-Square Triangles, which creates a good contrast with the swirls and curves of the floral patterns in the fabrics. Two of the fabrics also have a background stripe, which, when combined with the angles of the triangles within the block, has quite a dynamic effect.

Flower Basket

The basket pattern revealed in this traditional block relies on the contrast between "basket," "background," and "flower" fabrics. Simple to piece and yet relatively complex to look at, it's a great block for contrasting angles with floral fabrics. For block-making instructions see page 171.

Fabric Choices

1 | Tilda Winterbird Grandma's Rose, Blue

2 | Tilda Christmas House Grandma's Rose, Red

3 | Tilda Winterbird Vintage Ornament, Bluegreen

4 | Tilda Christmas House Rose Stripe, Red

5 | Tilda Winterbird Rose Stripe, Blue

Palette

10 Patterns and Plains

This is the largest palette of fabrics used in this book, to demonstrate how combining patterned fabrics with plain fabrics can itself form a pattern. By symmetrically placing the patterned fabrics and plain fabrics in the Nine-Patch block, the contrast between the two fabric types adds a sort of cross pattern to the square Nine-Patch block pattern. This effect has been explored further in the quilt on page 34.

Fabric Choices

| 1 | Denyse Schmidt Flea Market Fancy Legacy Medallion, Red

| 2 | Denyse Schmidt Flea Market Fancy Legacy Bouquet, Red

| 3 | Anna Maria Horner LouLouThi Triflora, Silver

| 4 | Kaffe Fassett Oriental Trees, Brown

| 5 | Denyse Schmidt Flea Market Fancy Legacy Posie, Gray

| 6 | Vintage cotton, pale terracotta

| 7 | Klona Cotton, Gray

| 8 | Klona Cotton, Ash

| 9 | Kaffe Fassett Shot Cotton, Bittersweet

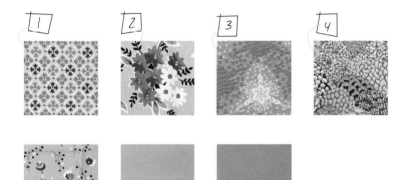

Nine Patch

One of the simplest blocks, the Nine Patch consists of nine equally sized squares. Often different colors or tones are used to create a sort of diagonal stripe effect, but here nine different fabrics are used, with the pattern within the block created by careful placing of the plains to contrast with the patterns. For block-making instructions see page 168.

Nine-Patch Cubed Quilt

Based on palette 10, this quilt takes the Nine-Patch block and amplifies it to form a whole quilt. Each small Nine Patch is part of a larger Nine Patch which is part of the overall Nine Patch—a sort of Nine-Patch cube or Nine Patch^3. The large range of fabrics has been pieced carefully so that all the solids form the small checkered effect of the smallest Nine-Patch blocks, and the patterned fabrics are kept as plain blocks.

You Will Need

- ❖ ¼yd Denyse Schmidt Flea Market Fancy Legacy Medallion, Red
- ❖ ¼yd Denyse Schmidt Flea Market Fancy Legacy Bouquet, Red
- ❖ ½yd Anna Maria Horner LouLouThi Triflora, Silver
- ❖ ¾yd Kaffe Fassett Oriental Trees, Brown
- ❖ Fat ⅛yd or if not available ¼yd Denyse Schmidt Flea Market Fancy Legacy Posie, Gray
- ❖ ¾yd 44in-wide vintage cotton, solid pale terracotta
- ❖ ½yd Klona Cotton, Gray
- ❖ ¾yd Klona Cotton, Ash
- ❖ Fat ⅛yd or if not available ¼yd Kaffe Fassett Shot Cotton, Bittersweet
- ❖ ¾yd Freespirit Designer Solids, Toast for the sashing
- ❖ 68 × 68in batting
- ❖ 68 × 68in backing fabric
- ❖ Terracotta quilting thread

Finished quilt size 62 × 62in

To Make the Quilt

1 Cut the fabrics for the blocks as follows:
❖ Denyse Schmidt Flea Market Fancy Legacy Medallion, Red: 4 × 6½in squares
❖ Denyse Schmidt Flea Market Fancy Legacy Bouquet, Red: 4 × 6½in squares
❖ Anna Maria Horner LouLouThi Triflora, Silver: 10 × 6½in squares
❖ Kaffe Fassett Oriental Trees, Brown: 16 × 6½in squares
❖ Denyse Schmidt Flea Market Fancy Legacy Posie, Gray: 2 × 6½in squares
❖ Vintage solid cotton, pale terracotta: 135 × 2½in squares
❖ Klona Cotton, Gray: 99 × 2½in squares
❖ Klona Cotton, Ash: 135 × 2½in squares
❖ Kaffe Fassett Shot Cotton, Bittersweet: 36 × 2½in squares

2 First piece the solids into 45 Nine-Patch blocks (see page 168 for block-making instructions). With a ¼in seam allowance, sew rows of 3, press seams, then sew 3 rows of 3 together. Arrange the fabrics randomly so that the different shades can be evenly distributed throughout the quilt.

3 Lay out the Nine-Patch and patterned blocks alternately in groups of 9, to form 9 squares, each with 5 Nine-Patch and 4 plain blocks within it. Arrange so that you are happy with the way the colors and patterns are distributed. Separate out each of the 9 sections slightly, and sew together 1 section at a time, sewing each row of 3 and then the 3 rows together. Repeat for each of the 9 sections so that you have 9 separate squares, each measuring 18½ × 18½in. Check measurements and trim to size if necessary.

4 Cut the fabric for the sashing to make strips as follows, joining strips to make the longer pieces where necessary:
❖ 6 strips measuring 2 × 18½in
❖ 2 strips measuring 2 × 57½in
❖ 4 strips measuring 3 × 62½in

5 Starting with the top row of 3 large blocks, pin and sew a 2 × 18½in sashing strip to each side of the central block, then pin and sew the top left block to the left piece of sashing and the top right block to the right piece of sashing, always with right sides together. Repeat for the middle and bottom rows so that you have 3 rows of 3 big blocks separated by the sashing.

6 Pin and sew the 2 × 57½in sashing to each side of the middle row of large blocks, then pin and sew the top and bottom rows to the top and bottom pieces of sashing. Trim any excess sashing from the edges. Pin and sew the 3 × 62½in sashing at each side of the quilt. Trim to the length of the quilt at each end, then pin and sew the top and bottom sashing in place. Trim ends.

7 See page 214 for instructions on how to make up your quilt and page 45 for information about quilting "in the ditch." See page 217 for binding instructions, and how to make binding from the offcuts of the plain and patterned fabrics.

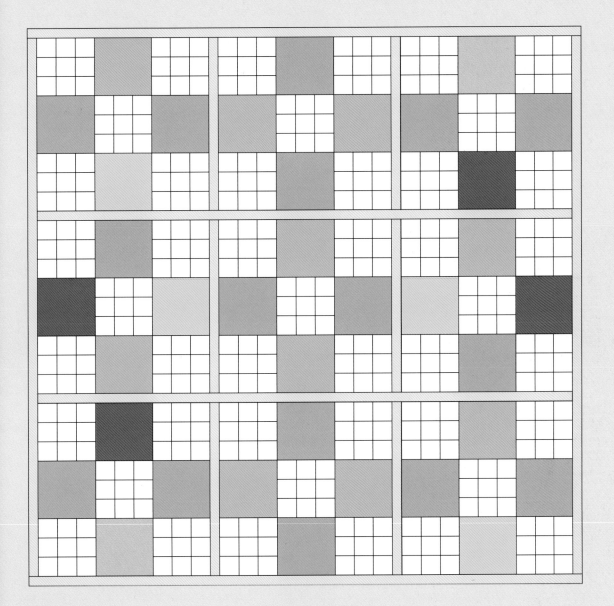

 Denyse Schmidt Flea Market
Fancy Legacy Medallion, Red

 Denyse Schmidt Flea Market
Fancy Legacy Bouquet, Red

 Anna Maria Horner LouLouThi
Triflora, Silver

Kaffe Fassett Oriental Trees, Brown

Denyse Schmidt Flea Market Fancy
Legacy Posie, Gray

Chapter

3 Adding Texture

By turning your beautifully colored and patterned patch-work creations into quilts or quilted items you instantly add the element of texture. This can be subtle if you quilt "in the ditch" between blocks, or it can be a feature if you use strong quilted patterns in contrasting thread. What will look best with your quilt? It depends on the colors and patterns and their overall effect, and the look you want to achieve, but the information and examples here should allow you to make the right decisions to create the textural effect that you want.

In addition to quilting, texture can be brought to a quilt with embroidery or appliqué, or by choosing textural fabrics to add a more three-dimensional element. Embellishments such as beads and buttons are simple additions that have great visual impact. You don't need to be heavy-handed with these elements; even small touches in a focal central block, for example, can add a whole extra dimension to your quilt. Consider some of the possibilities with the examples in the fabric palettes in this chapter, and you'll soon be making great textural choices along with your ideal pattern and color combinations.

Texture in Quilts

There are many different ways to add a textural element to your quilts, from the fabrics you choose to embellishment with beads and buttons, but the most basic one of all is the quilting itself. Without quilting, your pieced fabrics are simply patchwork, with only the seams between pieces adding a tiny hint of texture (assuming your fabrics are smooth cottons).

Quilting

The basic texture in any quilt comes from quilting the patchwork top, batting, and backing fabric together. This is influenced both by the thickness or "loft" of the batting and by the type of stitch and stitch pattern used to sew the layers together. Imagine a quilt in cross-section, with the backing fabric layer, batting layer, and quilt top like a layer cake. Tightly sewn machine stitches and batting with a high loft will make for a quilt with pronounced bumps where there is no stitching and ridges where the layers are held tightly together. By contrast, a thinner batting with low loft and looser hand-quilting stitches won't have too much difference in height between where the stitches hold the layers together and where the layers simply rest on top of one another.

Most batting will have a guide from the manufacturer for the maximum distance between your quilting, called the quilting interval. This can vary from 2in to 10in, so it's well worth checking before you buy, especially if you only wish to quilt at larger intervals.

Fabric Choices

Of course, not all fabrics are the smooth cottons so often used in patchwork and quilting. You can instantly add texture to your quilt by using textured fabrics—from coarse linens to heavy damasks and smooth velvets to elegant brocades, there are no limits to your fabric choices. However, do bear in mind that heavier-weight fabrics can be difficult to piece and cannot be washed in the machine, and it's always advisable to combine fabrics of a very similar weight. See page 30 for an example of a quilt block using unusual fabrics.

The battings shown here all have different properties, so it's worth shopping around and seeing samples before deciding which type will be best for your project. From left to right they are 100% polyester, 100% bamboo, and 80% cotton 20% polyester blend.

Fabric Effects

Fabric doesn't have to be pieced together as flat pieces. Many different effects are possible by adding tucks, pleats, ruches, and gathers, not to mention the vast range of appliqué techniques that can be employed. Manipulating fabric in interesting ways is something that you'll see on many art quilts, and in a sense there are no rules—play around and experiment with your fabric and see what effects you can achieve.

Embellishments

One of the great things about working with fabric is that you can sew things onto it for extra interest. Sewing beads around a fabric motif, adding little buttons at the joins between blocks or in the blocks themselves, and attaching ribbon or ric-rac are some of the more popular ways to add textural interest. You can add whatever you like to your quilt so long as it isn't so heavy that it pulls the fabric out of shape and it isn't so sharp that it could cut into the quilt top.

Buttons and beads are a pretty way to add a three-dimensional element to your quilt. They can be added to the blocks before assembling the quilt or once the quilt is made (though you'll see the stitching on the back). Be sure to attach embellishments extra securely if there are pets or small children around who may be tempted to chew on them.

Quilting Styles

There are a few different ways to stitch together the top, batting, and backing of a quilt, and each method creates a different effect. In essence, the quilting part of making a quilt is a practical way of attaching the three layers together at regular intervals so that the top, batting, and backing are held in position to create an even and stable quilt.

Thread types for hand-quilting include, from left to right, blue cotton perlé, white hand-quilting cotton, gray stranded embroidery thread, and cream cotton perlé.

Hand-Quilting

Perhaps the fastest and simplest way of securing the layers by hand is by "knotting" or "tying" the quilt. Knotted or tied quilting is achieved by sewing a stitch through the layers, then back again, and tying the ends of the thread together. Repeat at regular intervals, and hey presto! Your quilt is secure. It's best to use thick, strong thread for this method, and you can choose whether to make the knots a feature on the top of the quilt or hide them at the back. You can sew buttons or beads at regular intervals for a similar effect. See the quilt on page 50 for an example of hand-quilting.

Other popular forms of hand-quilting use lines of hand-stitching at regular intervals. These lines can be straight, curvy, decorative, or plain—the choice is yours. And of course, if not using a machine you have a greater choice of threads—thicker hand-quilting threads, embroidery floss, very fine yarn… So long as the chosen thread is strong and durable there are many options to choose from. See palette 13, page 46, for an example of hand-quilting using a Japanese Sashiko style, where the thread is in strong contrast to the fabric.

Machine-Quilting

The options for machine-quilting will depend on your sewing machine and your confidence. All machine-quilting involves some sort of running stitch, but stitch length and whether it's straight, zigzag, or a fancy stitch that can be programmed into the machine is up to you. Sewing straight lines is the most straightforward way to quilt by machine, but where you place those lines on the quilt top can make a big difference to the finished effect.

Quilting "in the ditch" (see palette 12, page 45) is a way to almost hide the quilting stitches as they lie in the seam between the blocks. Couple this with invisible thread and your quilting will be as subtle as it can possibly be. Quilting horizontal or vertical lines at close intervals will create a striped look (see palette 11, page 44), while quilting intersecting lines at different angles gives a refracted, geometrical appearance.

Of course, you don't have to stick to straight lines. Curves, concentric circles (see palette 14, page 47), waves, and flowing patterns are all possible when machine-quilting, but if the pattern you want to achieve has any tight curves, use a free-motion embroidery foot on your machine.

Long-Arm Quilting

This method of quilting involves a special sewing machine called a long-arm quilter. There are many companies offering long-arm quilting services, so check your local area to see what's available. You can choose the design, and the patterns achieved by this method are usually quite intricate and very even and regular.

Embroidery and Appliqué

There are many different kinds of embroidery and appliqué, and I've put them together here as they often go hand in hand, with appliquéd motifs featuring embroidered edges or embellishment. Adding an extra layer of fabric or creating a raised pattern with embroidery floss can really bring a quilt design to life and it is a simple way to add a focal point to the overall design.

If your embroidery skills are a little lacking, search out embroidered fabrics to piece together. There are many modern fabrics that have machine embroidery in their pattern. Or you could hunt down some vintage hand-embroidered cloths from thrift stores or your family and friends.

11 Parallel Lines

This palette and the following three share a range of five fabrics and the same Four-Patch block, but are all quilted in different ways. You can see that the overall effects are quite different in each block—and just imagine the effect when amplified over a whole quilt! Here, the parallel lines create a textural stripe. You can play around with the intervals between the lines of stitching, even varying them across a whole quilt.

Four Patch with Parallel Lines

The straight lines of the quilting work well with the straight lines in the block, creating harmony between piecing and quilting. It's important when quilting parallel lines to ensure they either line up with piecing seams or are at purposeful angles to them—otherwise your finish could look messy. For block-making instructions see page 164.

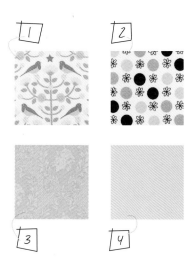

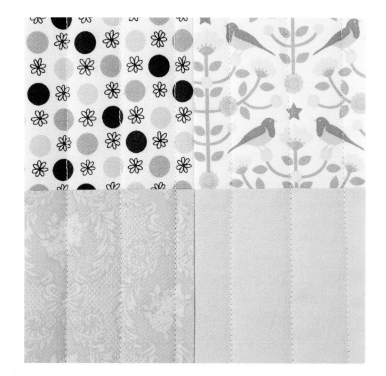

Fabric Choices

| 1 | Tilda Winterbird Folklore Bird, Blue

| 2 | Denyse Schmidt Flea Market Fancy Flower and Dot, Turquoise

| 3 | Tilda Winterbird Vintage Ornament, Light Blue

| 4 | Klona Cotton, Light Pink

Palette

12 In the Ditch

The quilting here has been machine sewn on the seams between the fabrics. Look closely and you can see the stitching, but imagine you are looking at a whole quilt—you wouldn't notice the stitching at all. If your machine sewing is prone to wander off target, use invisible thread—that way no one will be able to see your in-the-ditch quilting, even if it pops out of the ditch on occasion.

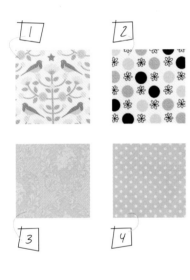

Four Patch in the Ditch

Because the quilting here is so unobtrusive it's the fabrics that you notice in this block, and the way they are pieced. In-the-ditch quilting is especially good if your fabrics have bold patterns that you don't want to interrupt with stitching. For block-making instructions see page 164.

Fabric Choices

 Tilda Winterbird Folklore Bird, Blue

2 Denyse Schmidt Flea Market Fancy Flower and Dot, Turquoise

3 Tilda Winterbird Vintage Ornament, Light Blue

4 Tanya Whelan Delilah Dots, Green

13 Sashiko Style

The bold stitches and contrasting embroidery floss used to quilt this block are reminiscent of Japanese Sashiko, where lines of running stitch are used to create simple patterns with white thread on indigo fabric.

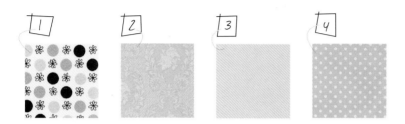

Fabric Choices

1 Denyse Schmidt Flea Market Fancy Flower and Dot, Turquoise

2 Tilda Winterbird Vintage Ornament, Light Blue

3 Klona Cotton, Light Pink

4 Tanya Whelan Delilah Dots, Green

Four Patch Sashiko Style

Concentric circles contrast well with the 90-degree angles of the Four-Patch block, and create a sort of "target" effect. This style of quilting can be used with straight lines or geometric designs. For more complicated stitching designs, mark the pattern out on your quilt top first—you can buy special fabric markers that disappear again, or very light pencil marks will be hidden by the stitches. For block-making instructions see page 164.

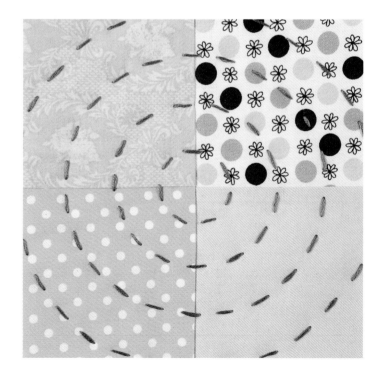

14 Curvaceous Quilting

Freehand machine-quilting mimics the effect of long-arm quilting, with curving lines of stitching forming a looping pattern. The only thing to watch out for when quilting curves and swirls is that the amount of stitching is fairly even across the quilt—if you have a very dense area of quilting lines on one side, your finished quilt could look unbalanced. Ensure, too, that any unquilted areas between your pattern of stitching aren't larger than the recommended quilting interval from the batting manufacturer.

Four Patch with Curvy Quilting

As with the block in palette 13, opposite, the curves contrast well with the "squareness" of the pieces in the block. For even more contrast you could use a colored quilting thread that is a deeper shade of one of the fabric colors, or for textural pattern without color interference, try an invisible thread. For block-making instructions see page 164.

Fabric Choices

| 1 | Tilda Winterbird Folklore Bird, Blue |

| 2 | Tilda Winterbird Vintage Ornament, Light Blue |

| 3 | Klona Cotton, Light Pink |

| 4 | Tanya Whelan Delilah Dots, Green |

15 Vintage Embroidered Cloths

Old table linen that has been lovingly hand-embroidered—but is now a little the worse for wear and rarely sees the light of day—is great for patchwork projects. You can cut your pieces according to where the embroidery is best, and cut out any stains, holes, or other marks in the cloth.

Fabric Choices

1 Piece from vintage linen table cloth

2 Piece from vintage fine cotton table cloth

3 Piece from vintage linen tray cloth

Crazy Patch

When working with vintage fabrics, you can often wind up with odd-shaped pieces in order to avoid holes or marks in the cloth. Crazy patchwork, where fabrics are pieced however you like, with no regard for regular angles or joins, is perfect for those little pieces that you want to use but won't fit into a more symmetrical pattern. For block-making instructions see page 213.

16 Appliqué and Embellishments

One of the simplest methods of appliqué is to use fusible web to stabilize the fabric for your motif shape, preventing any fraying at the edges. Iron the webbing to the wrong side of the motif fabric to reach just outside the outline of the shape, then cut out the shape. Once the motif is attached to the background fabric you can add decorative stitching to hide the raw edge, and add little embellishments to draw attention to the shape of the motif.

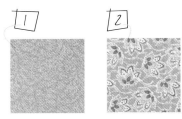

Fabric Choices

1 Feather pattern "blender" fabric in lilac

2 Fabric Freedom Hyde Park, Pink

Further ideas

Use a motif block as the central focus to a quilt, or add motif blocks at regular intervals throughout the design for a real wow factor.

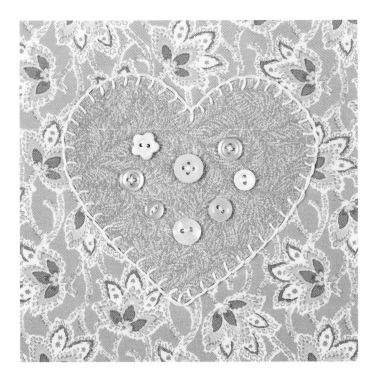

Appliquéd Motif

For any motif block, simply cut a piece of fabric the required block size for your quilt and choose a motif design that fits within it, leaving at least a ½in border all round. It's a good idea to make a template from thin card in case you want to use the motif again. The blanket stitch edging works well to add interest to the shape, and the buttons cheer up the plain fabric used for the heart.

Pieced Vintage Embroidery Quilt

I've been collecting vintage embroidered cloths for many years, always meaning to gather enough to make a large quilt for my bed. As all things vintage have become more popular it's been harder to pick up great pieces at reasonable prices, but I finally got there. One of the pieces is from my neighbor George, whose late wife May worked the embroidery. I don't know who the other embroiderers were, but I'm in deep admiration of their skill.

You Will Need

❖ A variety of vintage embroidered cloths. I used 3 large table cloths plus 2 tray cloths and a smaller piece that had been a wall hanging.
❖ ¼yd Klona Cotton in Mellow Yellow for binding
❖ ¼yd Klona Cotton in Peach for binding
❖ 86 × 63in batting
❖ 86 × 63in backing fabric
❖ White Cotton Perlé for ties
❖ Needle for hand-stitching
❖ White thread for machine sewing the binding

Finished quilt size 58 × 81in

Further ideas

You could make a quilt like this in any size, depending on the linens you have available and what the quilt is for. Simply piece the top to your desired size and design, then measure it, and buy batting and backing fabric slightly larger than the quilt top.

To Make the Quilt

1 First work out how the pieces for the quilt top are going to look best. I did this by folding my cloths in half and laying out half of the quilt from the center outwards, filling in smaller gaps with smaller tray cloths and working out where offcuts from larger cloths could be used.

2 Once your cloths are roughly in position, it's time to get brave with the scissors. Cut along your folds, leaving a generous seam allowance at this stage, if you can, of around 2–3in. Use the pieces that had been folded under to lay out the other side of your quilt, so that you have all of the pieces roughly in position.

3 When you have wiggled and jiggled, tucked under and folded over all of the pieces, and you're happy with the overall design, take a photo. The camera on your cell phone could be the easiest option—but whatever you use, it's a good idea to have a reference of how the pieces fit together before you have to move them to start pinning.

4 If it's possible, try to divide your quilt into vertical or horizontal strips by separating the fabrics slightly. The quilt here has three main sections—top, middle, and bottom—and I tackled each part separately before sewing all 3 together.

5 Choose the section that has the least seam allowance to start with. I started with the bottom section as this was the area I knew to have little "extra" fabric. Pin the pieces together where you want the seam to be, then trim seam allowances to ¼in. Move the pins if necessary and sew the section pieces together, pressing seams either open or to one side as you go.

6 Once you have completed a section that runs the width or length of your quilt top, measure it carefully. Use these measurements as the width/length of your quilt, and ensure all other sections fit with them.

7 Complete the other sections as in step 5, then sew your sections together. See page 214 for instructions on how to make up your quilt.

8 Once the quilt "sandwich" is pinned or basted together, use hand-quilting thread or embroidery floss to tie the layers together. Thread 3–4in thread through your needle, sew through the layers from back to front and back again, then knot the ends together securely at the back of the quilt. Repeat at regular intervals across the whole quilt, according to the recommendation on your batting. See page 217 for binding instructions.

4 Pretty Pastels

Light and summery, pastel colors are cheerful, pretty, and easy on the eye. They have the advantage of always looking harmonious together, whether you choose to use a large range or just a few shades, giving you scope to combine radically different fabric and block patterns without risking a horribly clashing quilt. Pastels are often seen as very feminine colors, but you can bring a masculine feel to a pastel palette by opting for cooler shades of green and blue, and choosing fabric and block patterns with a linear, geometric look.

All pastels combine well with white for a crisp freshness, or, if you're concerned about pastels looking insipid, use them with deeper tones for a more dramatic effect. Pastels are a traditional choice for babies, possibly because stronger colors can overwhelm their delicate features. If you want a baby quilt with a modern feel try the geometric look, as in the quilt at the end of this chapter, where solid pastel shades allow the block patterns to dominate and a square quilting pattern adds dynamism to an otherwise very simple design.

17 Lavender Flowers

When lavender blossoms the flowers always looks so pretty against the soft green foliage. The fabrics chosen for this palette evoke those colors but also add some slightly stronger shades in the Tend the Earth fabric. This gives the blocks more visual impact without overpowering the softer tones in the Field Study and vintage stripe fabrics.

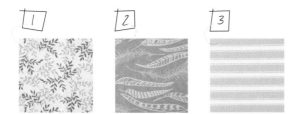

Trailing Star

This large block relies on three different colors or fabric in three distinct tones to show the Trailing Star pattern. The effect here is a subtle one due to the tonal similarity of the fabrics, but the pattern remains distinct. For a whole quilt you could try alternating Trailing Star blocks with plain blocks of each fabric, or adding sashing between the blocks to emphasize the block pattern. For block-making instructions see page 192.

Fabric Choices

1 Deb Strain Tend the Earth, pattern 19544

2 Anna Maria Horner Field Study Fine Feathered, Ghost

3 Vintage sage green and white stripe cotton

Economy Patch

The on-point angles in this square-within-a-square block have a dynamic visual effect. The softness of the fabric colors temper the block's dynamism to give a balanced overall effect that would look great repeated throughout a quilt or combined with other blocks. As the name suggests, there is no fabric wastage with this block so it's a thrifty choice. For block-making instructions see page 182.

Further ideas

If you like the look of a block but are worried it might be too fiddly to piece, try scaling it up and making it a central feature—or even your whole quilt. A giant Trailing Star, for example, would look fantastic as a lap quilt!

Bow Tie

This classic block is only a little more complicated than a basic Four Patch to piece, making it one of the faster and simpler of the classic blocks. You can play around with multiple Bow-Tie blocks to create different overall arrangements in your quilt. It's a great candidate for quilting in the ditch, which allows the block pattern to dominate. For block-making instructions see page 179.

18 Peach Melba

Peaches, pinks, and yellows come together with touches of cream here to create your very own fruity ice cream sundae of a color palette. The Liberty fabric packs more of a visual punch with its black outlines to the floral shapes, so use sparingly for a softer overall effect.

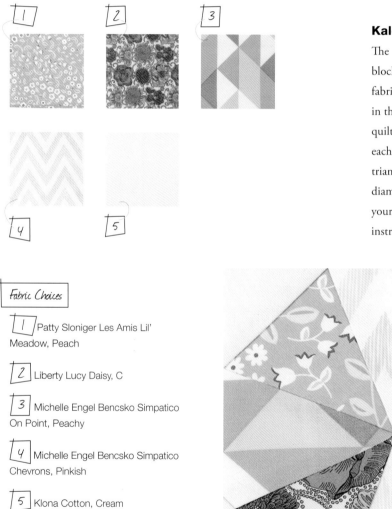

Kaleidoscope

The kaleidoscope effect created in this block allows for the patterns of each fabric to mingle, offset by the plain cream in the corners. Repeated throughout a quilt you would have an equal amount of each patterned fabric, with the cream triangles of each block merging to form diamonds of "ice cream" calm among your "peaches." For block-making instructions see page 196.

Fabric Choices

1 Patty Sloniger Les Amis Lil' Meadow, Peach

2 Liberty Lucy Daisy, C

3 Michelle Engel Bencsko Simpatico On Point, Peachy

4 Michelle Engel Bencsko Simpatico Chevrons, Pinkish

5 Klona Cotton, Cream

Broken Dishes

Using just two of the fabrics, this block helps create a strong contrast between the striking Liberty fabric and the softer pattern of the Patty Sloniger Les Amis. In a whole quilt you could create many different effects by simply varying the fabrics within the blocks for a scrappier feel, or keeping with only two fabrics as here for a more geometric look. For block-making instructions see page 166.

Melon Patch

Introducing curves creates a good contrast with the geometric patterns in the two Simpatico fabrics used in this block. What's more, the curved shapes are added using fusible web appliqué, so although it looks a little tricky to piece, it's basically just an embellished Four Patch. For block-making instructions see page 208.

Further ideas

The mélange of colors and pattern shapes in this palette would lend themselves really well to a quilt incorporating lots of different blocks for a jumbled effect. Try using a bunch of Four-Patch designs and play around with their arrangement so you get balance overall before sewing together for a quilt top.

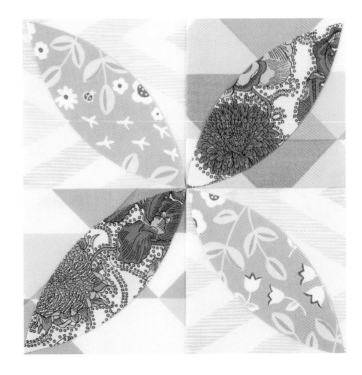

19 Ice Cream on the Sidewalk

Although no one likes the sound of a wailing child when their cone goes splat, the resulting mess can look quite lovely in terms of color! Inspired by this familiar summer sight of ice-cream aftermath, the pastels in this palette are set against a mid-tone gray reminiscent of concrete sidewalks.

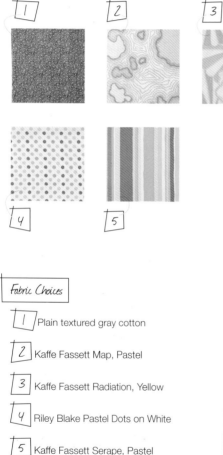

Nine Patch

With five fabrics in the palette, a Nine-Patch block is a great way to showcase all of the fabrics. The grid-like pattern is similar to the paving stones of European sidewalks and city piazzas, and would look great repeated across a whole quilt top, especially as the block is so straightforward to cut and piece. For block-making instructions see page 168.

Fabric Choices

1 | Plain textured gray cotton

2 | Kaffe Fassett Map, Pastel

3 | Kaffe Fassett Radiation, Yellow

4 | Riley Blake Pastel Dots on White

5 | Kaffe Fassett Serape, Pastel

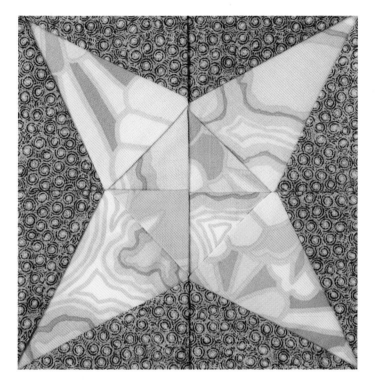

Windmill Star

Although a little time-consuming to piece as it uses triangle templates, the wonderful effect you can create with this block makes it worth the effort. Pale pastels in the "star" against the gray background look quite dramatic. If you didn't want to make a whole quilt from them, four of these blocks would make excellent focal points on a quilt top if used in the corners or together in the center. For block-making instructions see page 194.

Pinwheel

Made up of Half-Square Triangles, Pinwheels are quick to piece and always look good when two different tones are used. Here, the color of the light-toned pastels and absence of it in the gray make a very distinct pinwheel shape. For block-making instructions see page 168.

Further ideas

Here, only one gray fabric has been included in the palette, but this theme of pastels against gray would be a great way to use lots of different scraps of gray fabric if you have them in your stash.

20 Summer Sky

The clear blue of a summer sky is hard to beat, especially when combined with early morning sunshine. This palette suggests those colors of sunny mornings before the heat of the day really takes hold and the world feels fresh and new. The fragments of deeper blues in the Lizzie House fabric add tonal interest to an otherwise purely pastel palette.

1	2	3	4

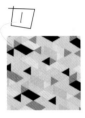

Fabric Choices

1 Lizzie House Constellations Supernova, Teal

2 Vintage cotton, pale blue with white star pattern

3 Klona Cotton, Baby Blue

4 Klona Cotton, Maize

Rail Fence

Using each of the fabrics in equal proportion, this block gives a dynamic yet balanced effect. You can play with the order of the stripes in each part—here, I changed the order around but for a more symmetrical look you could keep them the same. For block-making instructions see page 188.

Boxed Square

Setting a central square of yellow within the blue fabrics in this block is immediately evocative of the sun in the pale blue sky. Because the blues are quite different colors, with the vintage fabric blue a warm shade and the solid fabric a cooler blue, you'd get quite a good striped effect if you repeated the block throughout a quilt. For block-making instructions see page 186.

Attic Windows

This block would appear more three-dimensional if two tones of yellow had been used for the "inner window" parts, but the effect is still striking with just one tone. Although the amount of yellow in the Lizzie House fabric is minimal, the block design draws this out and helps balance the fragments of deep blue. For block-making instructions see page 191.

Further ideas

One of the fabrics in this palette is a vintage piece, but why not use all vintage fabrics? Men's cotton shirts from thrift stores are often available in an array of blues, and if cut into usable pieces can make great quilting fabric.

21 Pigs Will Fly

Taking pastels to one of their more vibrant places, this clean palette of pink and white is sweet and girly but not too babyish. The eye-catching patterns in the fabrics ensure the blocks here are fresh and fun. The blocks demonstrate a way to combine a pictorial pattern with other patterns that balance rather than fight with it.

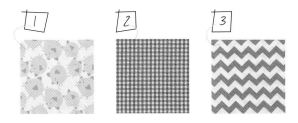

Fabric Choices

1 David Walker Fabrics Get Together 2

2 Riley Blake Small Gingham, Hot Pink

3 Riley Blake Small Chevron, Hot Pink

Half-Square Triangle

Half-Square Triangles are incredibly simple but are a great way to contrast two fabrics directly. Here, the contrast is all about the pattern as the fabrics share the same colors, but if you mix and match with other blocks or play around with arranging a whole group of Half-Square Triangles like this one, you'll soon be having fun creating a really interesting quilt. For block-making instructions see page 166.

Octagon

Octagons are a really good way of showcasing pictorial fabrics, in this case with the gingham "corners" framing the cute pigs design. Relatively simple to piece, they are a quick way of making a fabric statement and make excellent focal points in a quilt top. For block-making instructions see page 181.

Evening Star

If you love star blocks but want to make a feature out of the central fabric, then the Evening Star is a great choice. You could, of course, continue the central fabric into the points, but I've chosen to use the outer "star" as a frame for the central fabric to show a more intricate way of framing pictorial fabric than the Octagon block. For block-making instructions see page 176.

Further ideas

If this palette is a little too vibrant, try using fabrics containing a paler pink, or a mixture of shades of pink. You could also contrast the pink with cream or beige for a much softer look.

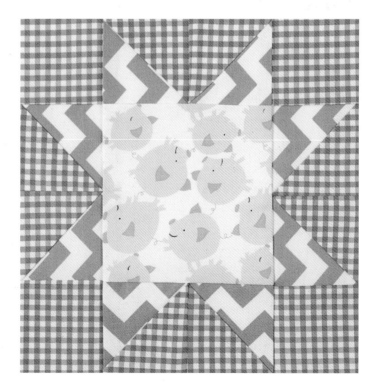

22 Sugared Almonds

The effect of using only solid colored fabric in a quilt can be a little too harsh, with the only pattern coming from the geometry of the blocks and the texture of the actual quilting. However, in these pastel colors, with a little white to add some tonal contrast, the result is quite easy on the eye. See page 68 for the full quilt based on this palette.

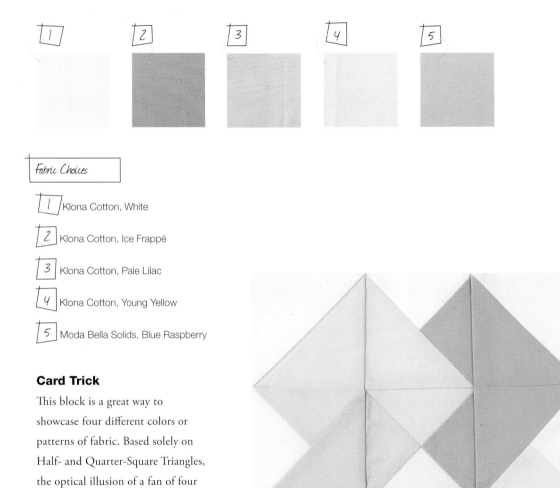

Fabric Choices

1 Klona Cotton, White

2 Klona Cotton, Ice Frappé

3 Klona Cotton, Pale Lilac

4 Klona Cotton, Young Yellow

5 Moda Bella Solids, Blue Raspberry

Card Trick

This block is a great way to showcase four different colors or patterns of fabric. Based solely on Half- and Quarter-Square Triangles, the optical illusion of a fan of four cards is achieved through careful placing of the different fabrics within what is effectively a Nine-Patch block. For block-making instructions see page 172.

Ohio Star

Simply pieced from plain squares and Quarter-Square Triangles, this is a straightforward block to make, again based on the Nine Patch. Here, the two colors used are tonally quite similar, which softens the star outline, but you could try different color combinations for a more eye-catching star. For block-making instructions see page 197.

Snowball

Snowballs are very plain blocks in themselves, but can look great when used together in a quilt top—or when combined with other blocks. They're a step up from a plain square and can provide a frame for embellishment, such as a section of intricate hand-quilting, embroidery, or appliqué, on the quilt itself. For block-making instructions see page 180.

Further ideas

Pastels hang so well together as a group of colors that you could bring in many different pastel solids to this palette for a really successful quilt design. If you don't want to use white for tonal contrast, what about a mid-tone of one of your pastel colors, such as a Mediterranean blue, or even a cool red?

Pretty Pastel Nursery Quilt

Soft pastel colors are always great options for the décor of a baby's room, with their calming hues and quiet cheeriness. More appropriate as a play mat for very young babies, whose bedding needs to be considered carefully to avoid overheating, this quilt would make a perfect gift for a new arrival and is large enough to last well into toddlerhood and beyond.

You Will Need

❖ ½yd Klona Cotton in White, or other solid white cotton at least 44in wide

❖ ½yd Klona Cotton in Young Yellow, or other solid yellow cotton at least 44in wide

❖ ½yd Klona Cotton in Light Lilac, or other solid lilac cotton at least 44in wide

❖ ¾yd Klona Cotton in Ice Frappé, or other solid pale green cotton at least 44in wide

❖ ¾yd Moda Bella Solids in Blue Raspberry or other solid pale blue cotton at least 44in wide

❖ ½yd Tilda Wintergarden Gingham, Teal for binding

❖ 43 × 60in batting

❖ 43 × 60in backing fabric

❖ White quilting thread

❖ Assorted pastel-colored quilting thread (you could also use sewing thread)

Finished quilt size 37 × 54in

To Make the Quilt

1 Cut fabrics for the quilt top as follows:
- White: 12 × 3½in squares, 12 × 3⅞in squares, 2 × 4¼in squares
- Yellow: 3 × 9½in squares, 2 × 3⅞in squares, 1 × 4¼in square, 8 × rectangles (3½ × 2in)
- Lilac: 3 × 9½in squares, 4 × 3⅞in squares, 1 × 4¼in square, 8 × rectangles (3½ × 2in)
- Green: 3 × 9½in squares, 16 × 3½in squares, 12 × 3⅞in squares, 3 × 4¼in squares
- Blue: 3 × 9½in squares, 16 × 3½in squares, 14 × 3⅞in squares, 7 × 4¼in squares

2 Set the twelve 9½in squares to one side as these are used whole when piecing the quilt top. The remaining cut pieces are used within the blocks. All 3½in squares are used as squares, so set these aside for each block (see diagram for reference). The 3⅞in squares are for Half-Square Triangles and the 4¼in squares are for Quarter-Square Triangles.

3 Make two Snowball blocks (see page 180). For each block you will need 5 white 3½in squares, then for the corner Half-Square Triangles 2 white, 1 lilac, and 1 green 3⅞in squares.

4 Make two Shoo Fly blocks (see page 169). For each block you will need 1 white and 4 blue 3½in squares, then for the corner Half-Square Triangles 2 white and 2 blue 3⅞in squares.

5 Make two Friendship Star blocks (see page 199). For each block you will need 1 blue and 4 green 3½in squares, then for the Half-Square Triangle elements 2 green and 2 blue 3⅞in squares.

6 Make two Ohio Star blocks (see page 197). For each block you will need 1 blue and 4 green 3½in squares, then for the Quarter-Square Triangle elements 1 green and 3 blue 4¼in squares.

7 Make two Card Trick blocks (see page 172). It is simpler to make a pair of these blocks, so for BOTH blocks you will need 4 white and 2 each of blue, yellow, lilac, and green 3⅞in squares for the Half-Square Triangle corners, plus the combined Half- and Quarter-Square Triangle elements. For the Quarter-Square Triangle parts you will need 2 white and 1 each of blue, lilac, yellow, and green 4¼in squares.

8 Make two Churn Dash blocks (see page 178) with the remaining cut pieces. Trim all blocks to measure 9½in square, then lay out all of the quilt top pieces as shown in the diagram. Pin and sew the blocks together in rows, then pin and sew the rows together. See page 214 for instructions on how to make up your quilt.

9 Once the quilt "sandwich" is pinned or basted together, thread your machine with invisible quilting thread and quilt in the ditch between the blocks. To add interest to the solid squares, use hand- or machine-quilting and coordinating quilting threads to create some textural interest. The quilt here has a freestyle square pattern sewn on the machine. See page 217 for binding instructions.

5 | Calm Neutrals

Neutral colors are often overlooked as a group as they are used so frequently as a tonal foil for brighter, cleaner, and more assertive colors. Add white or black to any palette and create a bit of super-crisp freshness or wow-factor drama; bring in a beige to calm down brighter colors or just add some nondescript "padding" to allow the other fabrics you've chosen to shine. Use browns or creams to add warm earthy tones to a palette, or add a dash of steely gray to balance out a fiery palette that's looking a little too hot.

But neutral shades, given the chance, can look great when combined, perhaps with just a dash of more defined "color" to keep things interesting, such as the touches of blue in palette 26 (see page 80). Understanding how neutrals can work with each other will help you to decide how best to use them with other colors, too. Like pastels, they always sit well together, and although their natural hues are gentle and calm, light and dark tones can be combined for a little drama, or a range of fabrics in similar tones can be assembled for a soft and soothing design.

23 Coconut

Crack open a coconut and this is the palette you'll get—the warm brown of the husk surrounding the rich deep brown of the shell with startling white coconut flesh on the inside. Because of the huge differences in tone, this neutral palette is fresh and vibrant, and if you wanted to use it for a quilt you could add in a plain white to your blocks for even more contrast.

Fabric Choices

1 Carolyn Gavin Village Green Dotty, Brown

2 Riley Blake Shades, Chocolate

3 Parson Gray Seven Wonders Wind, Crimson

Quarter-Square Triangle

Simple and straightforward, Quarter-Square Triangles are a great way of contrasting two fabrics from a palette in an interesting way. It's efficient to piece them in pairs, making two at a time, so bear this in mind when incorporating them into your quilt designs. For block-making instructions see page 167.

Triangle Hexagon

Six equilateral or 60-degree triangles can be grouped to form a hexagon shape, and if you want to make a hexagon quilt, this is a good way of adding extra interest to your blocks in a relatively uncomplicated way. This block looks great with two different fabrics—as well as with three, as here—but avoid a black and yellow combination unless you want people to think your quilt is radioactive! For block-making instructions see page 202.

Columbian Star

This large, intricate block is made up of diamonds and triangles to form a star within a hexagon. It works well with three tonally different fabrics, as here, to emphasize the star pattern created by the diamonds. Not for the fainthearted, it takes a little time but comes together quite easily if pieced in stages. For block-making instructions see page 200.

Further ideas

Any deep brown and white fabrics would work in this simple palette, and you don't need to be limited to three fabrics. The key to its freshness is the tonal contrast between the rich browns and cool, crisp white, so bear this in mind if you want to recreate the theme with your own fabric choices.

24 Fresh Oyster

There's something magical about seeing oysters in their shells, with the rough gray-brown exterior cracked open to reveal the creamy white oyster tinged with bluey gray, nestling in the smooth mother-of-pearl shell interior. A hint of blue goes well with the neutrals here, and warm and cool shades work together to add a little dynamism to the palette.

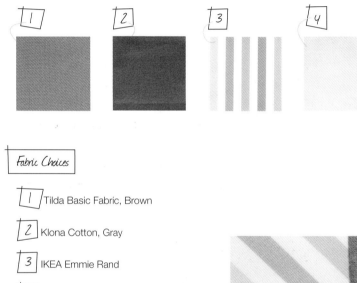

Fabric Choices

1 Tilda Basic Fabric, Brown

2 Klona Cotton, Gray

3 IKEA Emmie Rand

4 Vintage off-white linen

Nine Patch

This straightforward block allows the colors of the palette to take center stage. Interest is added by using the striped fabric on the diagonal, and aiming the stripes inward gives a strong directional feel. For block-making instructions see page 168.

Pinwheel

Half-Square Triangles can be used to great effect with fabrics that have a big difference in tone. Here, the pale stripes stand out well against the dark bluey gray and warm beige. The white fabric from the original palette hasn't been used in the block, but would look great as sashing between the blocks on a quilt top. For block-making instructions see page 168.

Further ideas

This palette would adopt a whole new feel if stripes and plains were replaced with curvaceous florals or subtle textures. Hunt around for soft patterns in these shades and you'll end up with a much subtler visual effect, no matter which blocks you choose.

Snail's Trail

Rather than using just two contrasting fabrics, I've relied on tonal difference here to create the Snail's Trail effect with all four fabrics, and started the block off with a Four-Patch square featuring each one instead of a plain square. The pattern could be continued using further rounds of triangles. For block-making instructions see page 183.

25 Sheepskin Rug

The texture of a natural sheepskin gives it a wonderful array of different creams and beiges that change with the light. The subtle patterns chosen in this palette are suggestive of the texture and colors of sheepskins, and as the color scheme is so soft and neutral, a quilt made from this palette would look great almost anywhere.

Fabric Choices

1 | Jennifer Young Katie Damask, Khaki

2 | 3 Sisters Luna Notte, B

3 | Riley Blake Shades, Cream

4 | Renne Nanneman Linen Closet, A

Crazy Patchwork

The subtle tones and patterns in this palette work well with the dynamic and random nature of Crazy Patchwork to create a crazy—but not too crazy—block. Use blocks like this to make the most of your fabric scraps, utilizing all those odd-shaped pieces from cutting other blocks and minimizing wastage. For block-making instructions see page 213.

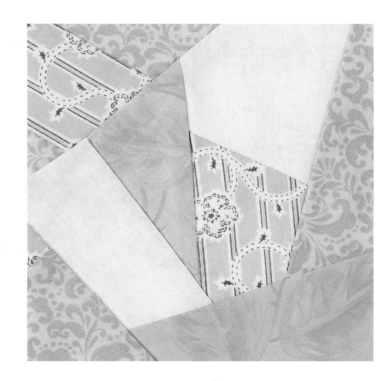

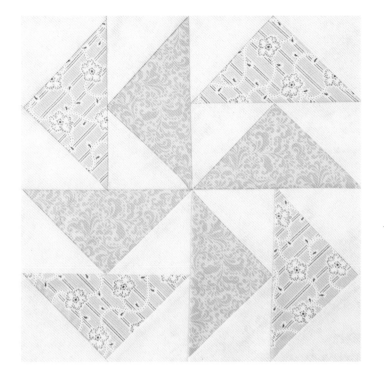

Dutchman's Puzzle

Based on the Flying Geese pattern, this block has a dynamic, directional look not dissimilar to a Pinwheel or Windmill. Although there is a fair amount of cutting, it's quite simple to sew together as not too many points need to be lined up. For block-making instructions see page 175.

Further ideas

A soft, neutral palette such as this one allows you to use strong, eye-catching blocks without creating a "loud" quilt. Conversely, keeping the patchwork too simple and subtle could result in a bland quilt, so make sure you choose carefully for the effect you want to achieve.

Love Ring

Curved seams work so well with the theme of curly, fluffy sheepskin, and by choosing just two of the fabrics, the tonal effect of the Love Ring block pattern can be seen clearly. Curved seams can be tricky to sew on the machine—if you're having trouble try hand-sewing them and machining the straight seams only. For block-making instructions see page 211.

26 | Winter Skies

Rain, hail, snow, sleet—perhaps not the most appealing weather conditions but a rich source of dramatic cloud patterns and colors, preferably viewed from the comfort of your own home through the window, of course. The mix of warm and cool grays in this palette gives a balance to the neutral colors, with hints of blue balancing the touches of brown and beige.

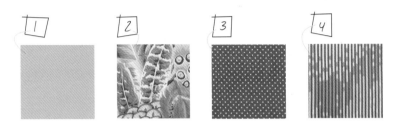

Fabric Choices

1 Klona Cotton, Ash

2 Philip Jacobs Feathers, Gray

3 Cotton polka dot, white on gray

4 Tula Pink Saltwater Sea Stripe, Aqua

Brick Wall

With 25 squares in total this block is great for showing little snippets of your palette fabrics. The staggered pattern created in the arrangement is enhanced here with the plain gray as the central diagonal, but you could play around with the fabrics and use one of the patterns here for a more subtle effect. For block-making instructions see page 165.

Le Moyne Star

Using just three of the palette fabrics, this block works well by setting the mid-tone patterned fabrics against the darker, more geometric polka dot. For a whole quilt you could vary where each fabric is used for visual interest, or mix star blocks with plain blocks for quicker results. For block-making instructions see page 193.

Grandmother's Flower Garden

This is a great block for showing off your fabrics, and although traditionally pieced by hand using the English paper-piecing method, hexagons can be sewn together just as successfully by machine (as here). This block is the basis for the quilt on pages 86–89, and you can see that the overall effect on a whole quilt is a lovely mélange of grays and browns and beiges. For block-making instructions see page 206.

Further ideas

The palette here only uses four fabrics but with this sort of color theme you could easily introduce more. Try to keep the warm and cool colors in balance and the patterns fairly abstract to retain the same look.

27 Cappuccino

The colors in this palette remind me of the swirls of milky froth and chocolate powder on top of smooth coffee—a warm and comforting collection of neutrals with the hit of rich chocolate brown giving some visual punch. Although the colors are all from the warm side of the spectrum, the palette has some good contrast within it due to tonal difference and also the difference in scale in the patterned fabrics.

Fabric Choices

1 Cotton damask pattern in brown and beige

2 Klona Cotton, Tan

3 Riley Blake Small Gingham, Brown

4 Free Spirit Designer Solids, Cream

Economy Patch

This block is a great way of framing a special fabric in an interesting way. The damask pattern in the center is a large-scale pattern so it lends itself to this treatment, while the plain tan and small-scale check act as a foil for its swirls and loops. For block-making instructions see page 182.

Broken Dishes

With two patterns and two plains in the palette, the Broken Dishes block allows for these to be paired up and contrasted with each other. Repeated across a whole quilt the solid and patterned triangles would create a strong refracted look, enhancing the block pattern even further. For block-making instructions see page 166.

Basket Weave

This is a very simple block to cut and piece, and multiple blocks can be arranged in a variety of ways across a whole quilt top. The strong contrast between the squares and rectangles is important to create an overall woven look once blocks are arranged together in a quilt. For block-making instructions see page 187.

Further ideas

With a large-scale pattern, such as the damask used in this palette, it's worth thinking carefully about the size of the fabric pieces in your blocks—if they are too small the pattern effect as seen on the fabric will be lost. Consider using blocks on a large scale, or choosing ones with some large areas within to show off your large-scale patterns.

28 Pale and Interesting

There is a huge range of subtle small-scale pattern fabrics available and they make excellent "fillers" for quilt tops, harmonizing with brighter colors and bolder patterns. However, they can also look sweet together, and lend themselves to blocks with small pieces as this won't detract from the fabric patterns. Consider using blocks such as these in combination with a color theme to add contrast, or use for a whole quilt for a classic, gentle effect.

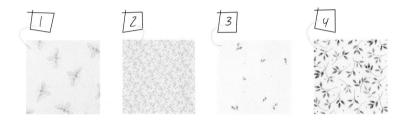

Fabric Choices

1 Renee Nanneman Linen Closet, 5487C

2 Renee Nanneman Linen Closet, 6094C

3 Maywood Studio American Beauty, 16

4 Maywood Studio American Beauty, 24

Four Patch

A classic palette such as this one deserves a classic block—and the Four Patch is perfect if you want simple cutting and fast piecing. Alternate with other blocks for additional interest, or repeat across a whole quilt for a really simple, sweet, and understated patchwork look. For block-making instructions see page 164.

Flying Geese

The directional nature of the Flying Geese "arrows" adds some dynamism to this soft palette. You can create lots of different patterns when combining Flying Geese blocks by rotating some of them, so play around and see what you can come up with. For block-making instructions see page 174.

Further ideas

The tiny prints on these fabrics would look great combined with other textural patterns such as batiks, marbles, and other mottled-effect fabrics as well as classic florals.

Courthouse Steps

This block is a variation of Log Cabin, and works well if you can divide your palette into two categories. Here, the effects are subtle as the fabrics are so similar, with "cream background" and "white background" as their main point of difference. For a bolder look you could use the fabrics from this palette combined with those from palette 22 (see page 66), or 33 (see page 100). For block-making instructions see page 185.

Simple Hexagons Quilt

Hexagon or "hexie" quilts have a reputation for being difficult and time-consuming to make, but they don't have to be. If you use relatively large hexagons and sew them together with machine-piecing, your quilt top will be done in an evening or two—especially if you use pre-cut hexagons!

You Will Need

- ¾yd Klona Cotton, Ash
- ¾yd Philip Jacobs Feathers, Gray
- ¾yd Polka dot cotton, white on gray
- ¾yd Tula Pink Saltwater Sea Stripe, Aqua
- ½yd 44in-wide solid pale blue cotton for binding.
  I used ¼yd each of two different shades.
- 48 × 51in batting
- 48 × 51in backing fabric
- Gray quilting thread

Finished quilt size 42½ × 45in

Further ideas

I've used really plain quilting here for a subtle and simple quilt. It would look great to add in more lines to echo all three of the angles of the hexagons, though, rather than just one. On some of the hexagons a lovely radiating pattern would be revealed, adding textural interest to the quilt. You could also add tiny mother-of-pearl buttons at the joins between hexagons if you wanted a more decorative look.

To Make the Quilt

1. If you are using the fabrics suggested and not pre-cuts then the best way to cut your fabrics is to make a hexagon template. You may be able to download and print one of the right size from the internet, otherwise you will need to make your own. The size I used is 7in wide and 6in high, plus ¼in seam allowance all around.

2. Once you have your template at the ready, you need to mark the hexagons on the back of each fabric. Butt the shapes up together and interlace them in the same way that the pieces are sewn together on the quilt to avoid wastage. You will need 16 hexagons of 2 of your fabrics, and 18 hexagons from your 2 other fabrics.

3. Cut the hexagons out very carefully, using either a rotary cutter or good dressmaking scissors. Your hexagons need to be very accurate if your quilt is to come together easily!

4. Arrange the hexagons according to the diagram opposite or in a pattern of your choice. I arranged them so that they were randomly scattered with no 2 pieces of the same fabric touching each other. When you are happy with the arrangement it's a good idea to take a photo, and to pin a note to the top left corner hexagon so you keep track of orientation.

5. See page 206 for advice on how to sew hexagons together in the Grandmother's Flower Garden block. I followed that approach, starting at one corner of the quilt, adding hexagons in diagonal rows until all were sewn together.

6. Press your quilt top carefully on the reverse. I like to press parallel seams in the same direction, alternating that direction as I turn the quilt. That way the corner joins open out into neat little flower shapes and lie really flat. Turn the quilt top over and press on the right side, encouraging any imperfect joins to line up nicely.

7. Trim the quilt top so that it has straight sides, and measure it. The top should be about 44 x 41½in, but don't worry if it differs, just alter your backing and batting sizes accordingly.

8. See page 214 for instructions on how to make up your quilt. Once the quilt "sandwich" is pinned or basted together, thread your machine with the quilting cotton and quilt in the ditch between the hexagons, sewing across the center of every third hexagon. See page 217 for binding instructions, using the solid blue fabric or fabrics for the binding.

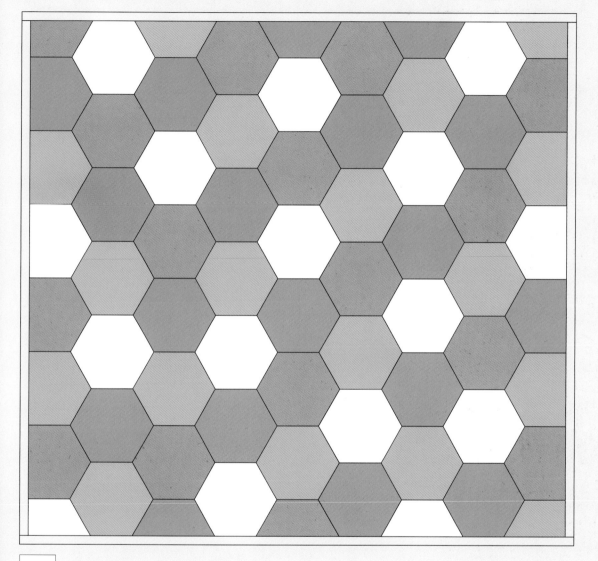

 Cotton polka dot, white on gray

Tula Pink Saltwater Sea Stripe, Aqua

Philip Jacobs Feathers, Gray

Klona Cotton, Ash

6 | Rich Colors

If a color looks as though it could burst with its own intensity it belongs firmly in this chapter—from deep, luscious hues of precious gemstones to the juicy natural shades of fall fruits and berries. Think chocolate, red wine, blackberries and plums, evergreen foliage and falling leaves—colors you want to wrap yourself in to keep out the cold.

If all this intensity is too much for your taste, try bringing some of the rich colors and patterns in the palettes here to softer shades. Little touches of intense magenta or royal blue can do wonders with a pastel palette, just as hot pinks or deep oranges can add a wonderful warm counterbalance to otherwise cool fabric combinations such as those in Chapter 7. Conversely, if you want to make a rich palette less intense, add a dash of neutral fabric to soften the effect.

The seasons can have a huge influence on our color preferences, so try looking at these palettes in the Fall or winter, and hopefully you'll be inspired by thoughts of cosy sweaters, log fires, and the evergreen trees and shrubs that come into their own at that time of year.

29 Peacock Feathers

The iridescent colors of a peacock feather are a beautiful combination of rich teal blues, jewel-like greens and warm ochers—a great balance of warm and cool colors. There are many different ways to explore this theme, such as finding some fabric with a peacock feather pattern as your starting point, or using a range of solids in peacock colors.

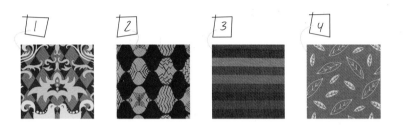

Fabric Choices

1 Patty Young Andalucia Birdie Damask, Navy

2 Parson Gray Curious Nature Empire Mark, Tailcoat

3 Kaffe Fassett Bold Stripe, Blue

4 Teal leaf pattern fabric

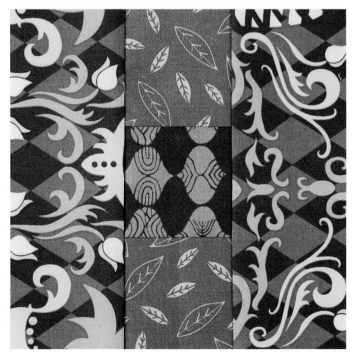

Boxed Square

This block reminds me of the "eye" pattern toward the top of a peacock tail feather, where deep, brownish greens are surrounded by bright bluish iridescence. You don't quite get the same effect here with matte cotton fabrics, but nevertheless it is a good way to contrast different colors within the palette. For block-making instructions see page 186.

Robbing Peter to Pay Paul

A great way to contrast two different fabrics. This block is simple to piece, though it does create a little fabric wastage. Imagine repeating the block across a whole quilt top—the effect could be quite hypnotic, especially with a stripe fabric such as the one here! For block-making instructions see page 179.

Further ideas

Fusible webbing is a great way to attach layers of fabric to your blocks without extra stitching, as used in the Grandmother's Fan block here. Just ensure that when quilting the layers together some of the quilting stitches secure any bonded fabrics in place.

Grandmother's Fan

This classic block is reminiscent of a fanned out peacock tail, and it's a great way of showing all four fabrics in the palette. The block itself requires templates and foundation piecing, so it's not for the fainthearted, but is worth the effort. The pieced fan can be appliquéd onto the background foundation fabric or, as here, ironed on with fusible webbing. For block-making instructions see page 209.

30 Wild Geranium

This palette is inspired by the wild geranium that bursts into bloom every year in my garden, producing masses of fuchsia pink flowers and bright green leaves for months on end. The color contrast between the flowers and foliage is quite a sight to behold, and seems especially attractive to bees!

Attic Windows

This simple block provides an effective way of framing one color fabric with another. Repeated across a quilt top it creates a wonderful three-dimensional effect, and you could always reverse the "window" and "frame" colors to create a sort of stripe. For block-making instructions see page 191.

Fabric Choices

1 Denyse Schmidt Chicopee Ladder Dot, Fuchsia

2 Joel Dewberry Heirloom Ribbon Lattice, Fuchsia

3 Denyse Schmidt Flea Market Fancy Eyelet, Green

4 Parson Gray Curious Nature Dimitri Vine, Pines

5 Michael Miller Heaven & Helsinki Wireframe, Citron

Log Cabin

This is the perfect block for two deeply contrasting colors, and it works really well when you have multiple fabrics in each colorway. There are plenty of different ways to arrange the blocks across a quilt top, too, giving you lots of scope for creating different patterns. See the quilt on page 104 for a diagonal stripe effect using this palette and block. For block-making instructions see page 184.

Chevron

Another eye-catching block, especially with such colorful fabrics! There is a fair bit of wastage when making a Chevron block due to the angled cuts, but staggering your straight strips before sewing them together can help to minimize this. For block-making instructions see page 190.

Further ideas

The brightness of this palette is due to the contrast between the magenta pinks and lime greens as well as the bright colors themselves. This is because they are opposite each other on the color wheel (see page 12). You could try different color combinations that sit opposite each other on the color wheel for a similar effect.

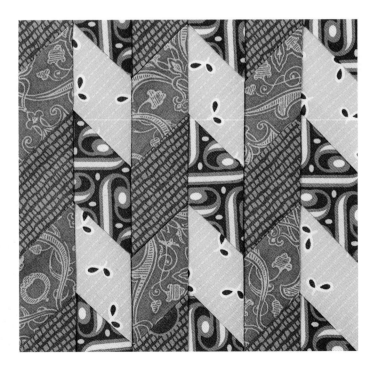

31 Treasure

The bright richness of jewel colors means they always look great together, so you can really go wild with the patterns that you choose to combine. In this palette the deep reds, hot pinks, and rich golds are balanced with the deep turquoise and purple, and the odd glimpse of paler shades within some of the patterns acts as a good foil for the main colors of the palette.

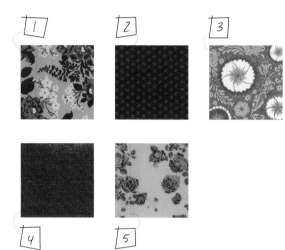

Rail Fence

This quick-to-sew block looks really effective with heavily patterned fabrics, especially when you group your strips in the same order for each block. Here, four of the five fabrics in the palette have been used so the strips didn't get too narrow, but there are no strict rules apart from keeping the widths even. For block-making instructions see page 188.

Fabric Choices

1 Joel Dewberry Heirloom Rose Bouquet, Gold

2 Kaffe Fasset Spot, Purple

3 Anna Maria Horner Good Folks Fortune, Sea

4 Klona Cotton, Crimson

5 Anna Maria Horner Garden Party Social Climber, Gold

Windmill

Mixing Half-Square and Quarter-Square Triangles makes for a lovely effect here. By only using the plain red and the red/purple polka dot fabrics for the Half-Square Triangles, the patterns work with the colors to create the visual effect of a windmill. For block-making instructions see page 170.

Further ideas

You don't need to limit a jewel-color palette to five fabrics, and in a sense the more rich-toned, deep-colored patterns and plains you can bring together, the better. Just be sure to choose a mixture of warmer and cooler colors for balance.

Six-Sided Star

Made up of six diamonds, this star-within-a-hexagon block would make a great centerpiece to a quilt made from cut hexagons, or if you don't mind lots of piecing you could make a whole quilt from blocks like this, alternating the colors from the palette. Here, just the gold-patterned fabrics have been used for the diamonds, set off by the surrounding deep turquoise. For block-making instructions see page 198.

32 | Spanish Tiles

Rich terracotta, off-white, and Mediterranean blue is a color combination that always makes me think of the gorgeous handcrafted tiles and other ceramics from Southern Europe, especially Spain. You could bring in other rich colors too but keep to natural tones such as pine green or ocher yellow to maintain the same theme.

Jacob's Ladder

The complementary colors in the palette work well with this block, bringing out the "ladder" nature of the pattern. I opted to exclude the solid cream fabric in order to have a very rich, intense overall look, but you could lighten things up by swapping out the solid blue or one of the patterned fabrics for the cream. For block-making instructions see page 173.

Fabric Choices

1 | Klona Cotton, Royal

2 | Liberty Tana Lawn Lodden, D

3 | Carolyn Friedlander Architextures Crosshatch, Tangerine

4 | Rashida Coleman-Hale Tsuru Old Lace, Vermillion

5 | Free Spirit Designer Solids, Cream

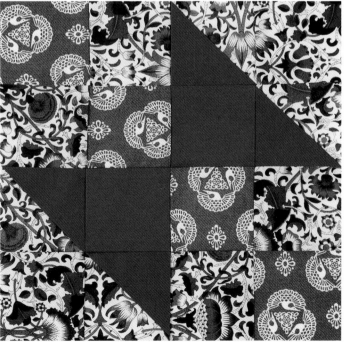

Churn Dash

Perfect for putting a big range of fabrics together, this block balances the five palette fabrics really well. If you combined a number of these Churn Dash blocks you'd have diamonds of cream to break up the richly colored central parts of each block. For block-making instructions see page 178.

Streak o' Lightning

This block showcases the complementary colors and the tonal difference that the solid cream brings. If you want a less dramatic effect, substitute the solids for the patterned fabrics and the "zigzag" nature of the block will be a little less loud! For block-making instructions see page 189.

Further ideas

Taking inspiration from holidays or places you'd like to visit is always rewarding—the hardest part can be narrowing down your color or pattern inspiration to create a cohesive palette. Keeping it simple is usually the most successful approach; separate your ideas into more than one quilt design rather than squashing everything together.

33 Red Wine

From claret to burgundy, red wine comes in an array of rich red and purple colors that make a deep, comforting palette for a quilt. This is another palette that would work brilliantly with a big range of fabrics sharing a deep red or purple theme, so raid your stash and see what you can put together.

Fabric Choices

1 Joel Dewberry Heirloom Tile Flourish, Garnet

2 Michael Miller Cora, Jewel

3 Stof 123 Play, 12

Flying Geese

This a great block to use with multiple fabrics from the same color range—you can vary the large triangles and keep the same fabric for the background triangles, which will give your quilt cohesion without limiting the fabric possibilities. Play around with the arrangement of the blocks for different visual effects for your quilt. For block-making instructions see page 174.

Melon Patch

For this block I've harnessed the tonal difference that the stripe fabric brings to the palette. The paler colors within the stripe give an overall effect of a mid-tone, although the deeper colors are in keeping with the theme. Because of this the curved shapes "pop" for an eye-catching effect. Try quilting around the outline of the patches to add further emphasis. For block-making instructions see page 208.

Further ideas

You could take the idea of tonal difference utilized in the Melon Patch block much further with this palette, adding in more mid-tone fabrics in deep pinks, lilacs, and mauves for a fresher look. If you make sure that you keep the colors on the warmer side of the color wheel and you don't stray too far into pastel territory, the palette should hang together well.

Shoo Fly

Unlike the Melon Patch block, this one uses the difference in pattern of the two fabrics for its contrast, rather than difference in tone. The small-scale geometric pattern is offset by the large-scale curved pattern and vice versa, creating a block that is quite subtle yet still has good visual impact. For block-making instructions see page 169.

34 Rich

The combination of rich chocolate brown with deep jewel colors conjures up thoughts of luxurious chocolates, opulent furnishings, and late-night candlelit dinners. The deep pinks, reds, and turquoises give a brightness to the palette while retaining its rich hues, so the overall effect on a quilt would be colorful, yet deep.

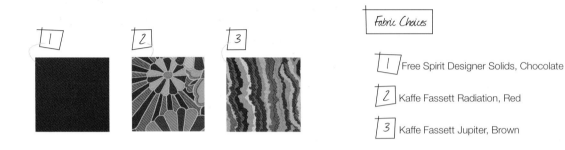

Fabric Choices

1 Free Spirit Designer Solids, Chocolate

2 Kaffe Fassett Radiation, Red

3 Kaffe Fassett Jupiter, Brown

Triangle Hexagon

These hexagons are a great way of repeating three different fabrics, and a whole quilt made from a combination of Triangle Hexagons and plain hexagons of the same size from the individual fabrics would look great. Piecing hexagons doesn't need to be difficult—so long as your cutting and seam allowances are accurate, they should come together easily whether you choose to machine-piece or use the traditional English paper-piecing method. For block-making instructions see page 202.

Bow Tie

Because I've used just the patterned fabrics in this block, the actual bow tie pattern is fairly subtle. For a stronger look you could contrast the solid brown with one of the patterned fabrics. Bow-Tie blocks work well with other blocks too—look for those based on a Four-Patch geometry for best results, such as Broken Dishes or Melon Patch. For block-making instructions see page 179.

Further ideas

When blocks lend themselves to being combined with others, it's a good idea to sketch out an overall quilt design on paper or on the computer. Think about whether you want your quilt to be symmetrical or to have a more haphazard, scrappy look, and arrange the different blocks accordingly.

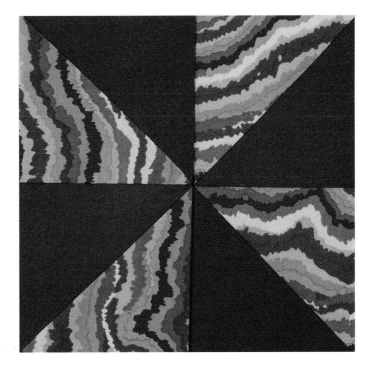

Pinwheel

Unlike the Bow Tie block, this block utilizes the visual difference between solid color and pattern, and so the pinwheel pattern of the block is quite striking. Again, this is a block that combines well with others based on a Four-Patch geometry, so try combining with other blocks to create your own quilt design. For block-making instructions see page 168.

Wild Geranium Log Cabin Quilt

Based on palette 30 (see page 94), this is a small lap quilt with a big personality—bright pinks and purples with acid greens make for a color scheme that couldn't get much brighter. If you want to make a larger quilt, simply add more blocks—remembering to recalculate the batting and backing amounts you will need as well as the fabric for the quilt top and binding. I've used a concentric circle pattern for the quilting as I like the way it contrasts with the angular nature of the blocks, but quilting in the ditch or with diagonal lines would also look great.

You Will Need

- ❖ ¼yd Denyse Schmidt Flea Market Fancy Eyelet, Green (A)
- ❖ ¼yd Parson Gray Curious Nature Dimitri Vine, Pines (B)
- ❖ ½yd Michael Miller Heaven & Helsinki Wireframe, Citron (this includes fabric for the binding) (C)
- ❖ ¼yd Maywood Studio American Beauty, 14 (D)
- ❖ ½yd Joel Dewberry Heirloom Ribbon Lattice, Fuchsia (E)
- ❖ ½yd Denyse Schmidt Chicopee Ladder Dot, Fuchsia (F)
- ❖ 37 × 47in batting
- ❖ 37 × 47in backing fabric
- ❖ Green quilting thread

Finished quilt size 31 × 41in

Further ideas

The colors used in this quilt are from directly opposite sides of the color wheel (see page 12), making this a complementary color scheme. If you like the bright contrast of this quilt but don't like the colors, try choosing another two colors from opposite sides of the wheel.

To Make the Quilt

1 Cut the fabrics for the blocks as follows:

❖ 2½in squares: 2 × A; 2 × B; 6 × C; 2 × D; 6 × E; 6 × F

❖ 2½ × 4½in rectangles: 4 × A; 4 × B; (no C); 4 × D; 8 × E; 4 × F

❖ 2½ × 6½in rectangles: 2 × A; 2 × B; 4 × C; 4 × D; 8 × E; 4 × F

❖ 2½ × 8½in rectangles: 4 × A; 2 × B; 4 × C; 2 × D; 6 × E; 6 × F

❖ 2½ × 10½in rectangles: (no A, B, C, or D); 5 × E; 7 × F

2 Separate your squares and rectangles by size and by color. Make 12 Log Cabin blocks (see page 184 for block-making instructions), varying the fabrics as you sew the pieces together, so there is variety within each block.

3 Press each block and check each one is 10½in square, trimming edges where necessary. Lay the blocks out and arrange them to form a diagonal stripe pattern as here (see diagram opposite), or other pattern of your choice. When you are happy with the arrangement it's a good idea to take a quick photograph for reference.

4 Starting at the top, sew the blocks together in rows. Press these seams in the same direction on each row, but alternate the direction from row to row so that they nest together in the next step.

5 Sew each row of blocks together, nesting the seams for a neat finish. Press the seams.

6 See page 214 for instructions on how to make up your quilt. Once the quilt "sandwich" is pinned or basted together, thread your machine with quilting cotton and quilt in the ditch horizontally between the main blocks (see page 45 for more information). Then, on the quilt back, mark concentric circles, leaving a margin of 4–6in between each, and quilt along these lines. As you are quilting on the back you will need to have quilting cotton in your bobbin for it to show on the front. See page 217 for binding instructions, using the remaining Heaven & Helsinki fabric for the binding.

 (A) Denyse Schmidt Flea
Market Fancy Eyelet, Green

(C) Michael Miller Heaven &
Helsinki Wireframe, Citron

 (E) Joel Dewberry Heirloom
Ribbon Lattice, Fuchsia

 (B) Parson Gray Curious
Nature Dimitri Vine, Pines

 (D) Maywood Studio
American Beauty 14

 (F) Denyse Schmidt Chicopee
Ladder Dot, Fuchsia

7 Cool Hues

The palettes in this chapter are all anchored in the blue side of the color wheel (see page 12), with cool purples, blues, mint greens, and crisp, cooler yellows working together to create clean, fresh color and pattern combinations. The colors mean that these palettes are some of the more masculine in the book, but you could always balance that with your fabric and block pattern choices. Bring in florals and curvaceous patterns to these palettes for a great balance of masculine and feminine.

Many of the colors in the fabrics featured here are purer versions of the cooler pastel shades in Chapter 4; combining elements of the pastel palettes with the palettes in this chapter could create some really gorgeous results. If the combinations in this chapter are looking a little shiveringly cold to you rather than pleasingly cool, try bringing in some warm colors such as reds, oranges, or pinks. Alternatively, you could heat up any of the palettes by adding warm neutrals such as beige or cream.

Sunny Morning

Inspired by those early days of summer when sunny mornings still have a chill in the air, the blues, yellows, and touch of grass green here are sure to put a spring in your step. It's not only the colors that give the palette a crispness; the linear nature of the patterns also helps with the overall cool look.

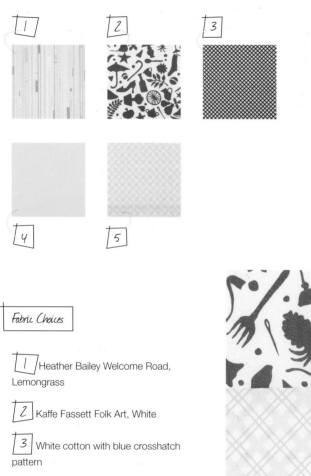

Nine Patch

I've arranged the fabrics in this Nine-Patch block in diagonal stripes, with the idea that this could be carried across a whole quilt top to give a dynamic, graphic look. Alternatively, blocks like this could be arranged so that the diagonal stripes appear to radiate out from a central point, creating an overall diamond pattern. For block-making instructions see page 168.

Fabric Choices

1 Heather Bailey Welcome Road, Lemongrass

2 Kaffe Fassett Folk Art, White

3 White cotton with blue crosshatch pattern

4 Free Spirit Designer Solids, Lemon

5 Tanya Whelan Delilah Picnic Check, Blue

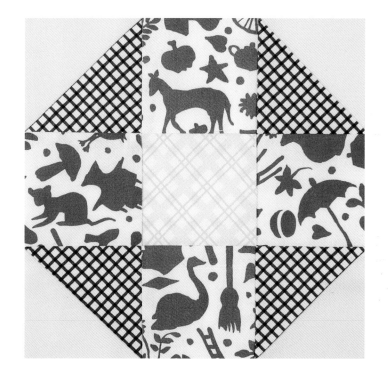

Snowball

This is quite an untraditional take on the Snowball block, as the fabrics forming the central "snowball" are varied, creating a pattern within. However, the blues in the central squares and triangles contrast well with the outer solid yellow, so the Snowball pattern remains distinct. This block combines well with the Nine Patch here and a quilt made from alternating these two blocks would look great. For block-making instructions see page 180.

Grandmother's Fan

This block has always reminded me of stylized images of radiating sunshine, so with a palette called Sunny Morning I couldn't resist putting the two ideas together. I've used fusible web appliqué to attach the fan to the background fabric; the quilting will attach the layers together more firmly. I like the way the strong pattern of the background fabric shows through the fan slightly, but you could add in a layer of plain white or yellow fabric between to prevent this show-through. For block-making instructions see page 209.

Further ideas

The radiating sunshine idea behind the Grandmother's Fan block could be applied in a more abstract way across a whole quilt using Nine-Patch blocks. Start off with predominantly yellow blocks in the lower left-hand corner, and gradually introduce more blues as the blocks head toward the top right corner, finishing with predominantly blues in that top right area.

36 Hoar Frost

The muted, subtle colors of the countryside after a heavy frost can be simply breathtaking. The gray-greens, turquoise tones and palest yellows mixed with soft gray in this palette emulate the landscape in those precious minutes before the sun garners enough strength to melt away the hoar frost coating on the fields.

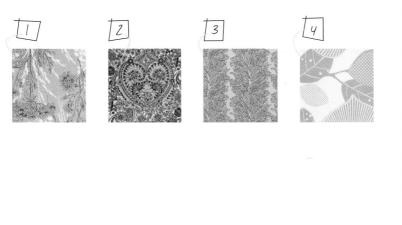

Art Square

This block is very similar to the Evening Star block, but the Flying Geese units at each edge are turned to point outward instead of inward, giving a square within a square effect. It works well here to frame the floral silhouette fabric, which has been fussy-cut to show at least one complete flower head. For block-making instructions see page 177.

Fabric Choices

1 | Floral silhouette pattern fabric in gray, powder blue, white and olive

2 | Liberty Tana Lawn Kitty Grace, D

3 | Parson Gray Curious Nature Coral Reef, Darkwater

4 | Amy Butler Midwest Modern Optic Blossom, Linen

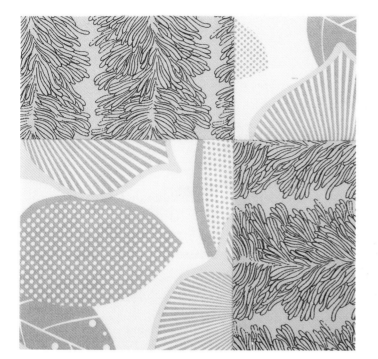

Basket Weave

The subtlety of the palette is lost a little in this block as the two fabrics with strongest contrast have been chosen. A quilt made from this arrangement would be very graphic. For a softer effect, you could vary the palette fabrics across the Basket Weave blocks, creating a more variegated quilt. For block-making instructions see page 187.

Further ideas

This color palette would work really well with a randomly pieced, scrappy quilt top. So long as the colors and tones were reasonably evenly distributed across the quilt you could use a wide range of fabrics in a range of sizes, letting the colors alone hold the design together.

Windmill

The choice of fabrics here makes the windmill effect fairly subtle, and would create a soothing quilt that remained true to the soft tones of the palette. Varying the fabrics used in the Half-Square Triangles and Quarter-Square Triangles would "tone down" the block pattern across the quilt even further for a lovely dappled look. For block-making instructions see page 170.

Violet Candy

Cool purples and pale lilacs provide a good tonal contrast in this palette, allowing for some great effects with the quilt blocks. The pale lilacs are subtly textured, whereas the deeper purples have plenty of pattern going on too, further distinguishing between the two aspects of cool purples chosen.

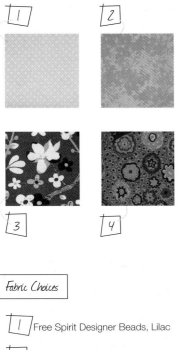

Courthouse Steps

This is an ideal block pattern to use when your chosen fabrics can be divided into two distinct groups. Here it's a simple matter of "dark" and "light," but the block would also work well with two contrasting or even complementary colors. Mixing Courthouse Steps blocks with Log Cabin blocks that have the same strip width and overall dimensions would look great. For block-making instructions see page 185.

Fabric Choices

1 | Free Spirit Designer Beads, Lilac

2 | Free Spirit Designer Fresco, Purple

3 | Kate Spain Good Fortune Tranquility, Waterfall

4 | Kaffe Fassett Millefiore, Blue

Drunkard's Path

This block pattern looks its strongest when the chosen fabrics have a good contrast, so I've used fabrics from the palette that do just that. Not only is light lilac contrasted with deep blue-purple, but a quiet pattern is up against a loud fabric design, which all works together to make the Drunkard's Path pattern all the clearer. For block-making instructions see page 210.

Further ideas

If you want to add in a greater variety of colors to this palette, try picking out a shade or tone of one used already within the patterned fabrics. That way, the palette will still hold together.

Octagon

By using both of the lilac fabrics for the corners, the simple Octagon block pattern looks reasonably interesting. If this variation were carried throughout a whole quilt, alternating lilac fabric centers with deep blue-purple centers and varying fabrics in corners, quite an intricate effect could be achieved from what is essentially a very plain block. For block-making instructions see page 181.

38 Swimming Pool

The different blues and turquoises that can be seen in a rippled swimming pool always seem to look stunning together, and this palette is a more exaggerated, stylized version of that effect. Touches of white in the fabric patterns remind me of the way light can dance over the ripples, as does the silver sparkle in the wax print fabric. See page 122 for the quilt made from this palette's fabrics.

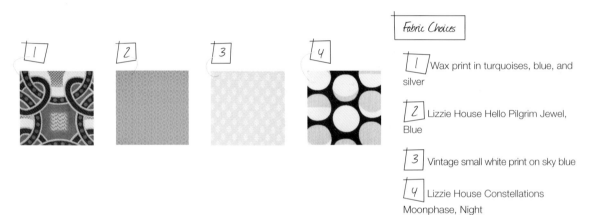

Fabric Choices

| 1 | Wax print in turquoises, blue, and silver

| 2 | Lizzie House Hello Pilgrim Jewel, Blue

| 3 | Vintage small white print on sky blue

| 4 | Lizzie House Constellations Moonphase, Night

Four Patch

Simple and quick to piece, the humble Four Patch can work with many different blocks, or even on its own for a traditional patchwork look. Here, the fabrics have been grouped into "small pattern" and "large pattern" and linked diagonally, but could easily have been grouped as "turquoises" versus "blues" instead. Alternatively, you could just choose two different fabrics for the block for a better diagonal contrast. For block-making instructions see page 164.

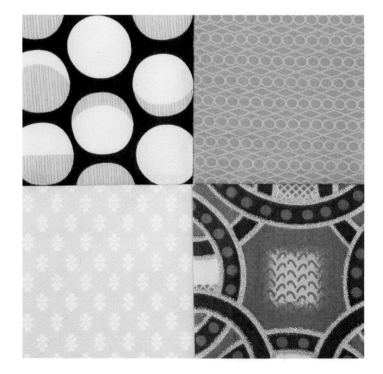

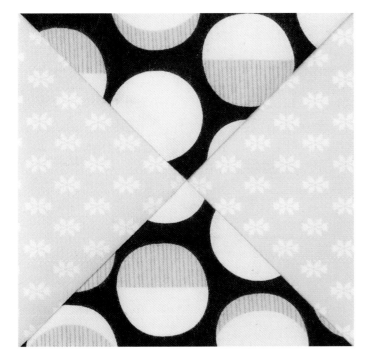

Quarter-Square Triangle

These blocks can be arranged together in a multitude of ways to create different visual effects. They can be easily pieced from Half-Square Triangles, and if you get a production line going with them they come together speedily. The angular nature of the block is best realized with fabrics that have a good contrast. For block-making instructions see page 167.

Inner City

This visually interesting block looks best when a big group of them are tessellated, creating a three-dimensional look not dissimilar from Tumbling Blocks. The effect relies on using three different tones, as here, and the pieces are all half hexagons. For block-making instructions see page 204.

Further ideas

There's no need to limit this palette to four fabrics. If you want to create a more varied look, just be sure to keep to the very limited colors used here in order to retain the true swimming pool color theme. Adding in more patterns will work well, but be careful not to mix too many styles.

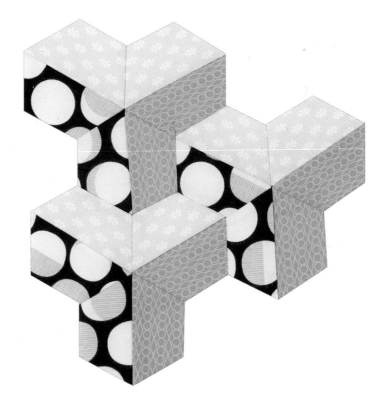

Fresh Mint

Shades and tones of mint green always look great together and if you add a dash of white to the palette you'll have a fresh, vibrant color collection that will make a great quilt. The Eleanor Grosch fabric used here gives the palette a childlike theme, but substitute a more abstract green pattern for a more mature look!

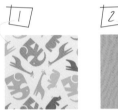

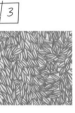

Fabric Choices

1 Eleanor Grosch Zoo Menagerie, Green

2 Free Spirit Designer Solids, Lime

3 Steffie Brocoli In the Forest Foliage, Green

Evening Star

Evening Star is very similar to Art Square, but in this case the Flying Geese units point inward to give the star shape. The block works well here to frame the stylized zoo animals in the central fabric, whose multiple shades of green hold the palette together. For block-making instructions see page 176.

Economy Patch

This block works even more obviously to frame the central Zoo Menagerie fabric, and here I have chosen a very specific part of the fabric so that the focus of the block is on the elephant. Fussy cutting is a good way to make the most of pictorial fabrics but can be a little wasteful. For block-making instructions see page 182.

Further ideas

This palette is almost exclusively green, but you could successfully introduce a highlight color to add a real wow factor. For the most dramatic effect try a pink from the opposite side of the color wheel (see page 12), or try a blue or a yellow, both of which would look great.

Half-Square Triangle

Sometimes keeping it simple can have the most dramatic effect. Using a Half-Square Triangle to contrast a solid fabric with a patterned fabric always looks really striking. This would look great repeated across a whole quilt, especially if only the patterned fabric was alternated. A less dramatic effect could be achieved by opting for as much fabric variation in the blocks as possible. For block-making instructions see page 166.

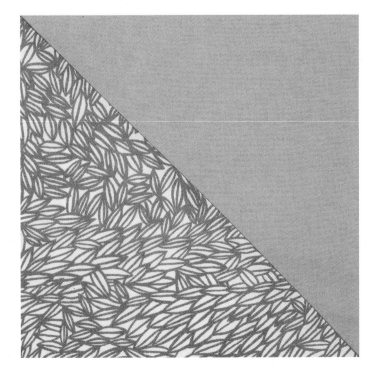

40 Color Free

What, no color? Monochrome quilts can look fantastic so long as there is enough pattern and tonal variation to make them interesting. Therefore, the fabrics chosen here are all very different in style. Combining so many styles might look too random with color in the mix, but it works well with black, gray, and white.

Fabric Choices

1 Lucie Summers Summersville Floral Scandi, Black

2 Batik cotton in black and pale gray

3 Ty Pennington Wave, Charcoal

4 Marimekko Ornamentti Satula

Kaleidoscope

I've used all four of the palette fabrics here and the kaleidoscope effect is a little lost as there is so much going on with clashing patterns. The Lucie Summers fabric dominates due to its simplified lines and warm creamy white background. Across a whole quilt this effect could be used to advantage by rotating alternate blocks, but if Kaleidoscopes formed part of a bigger overall design it would be better to limit the fabrics used to two or three. For block-making instructions see page 196.

Rail Fence

This block shows a much more successful combination of all four fabrics—the overall effect is of dappled tone and pattern lines. Combining Rail Fence blocks with plain squares of each fabric would create a really interesting quilt, allowing each pattern to be shown in full. For block-making instructions see page 188.

Further ideas

With this palette you could throw in as many black, white, and gray fabrics as you have in your stash for the best results. And if you want to give the monochrome look a tiny little lift, try binding the quilt in a really bright color—hot pink or acid green would look great.

Broken Dishes

Here, just two of the fabrics have been contrasted so that the block pattern is reasonably apparent. However, the strong and contrasting patterns of the fabrics do distract from the Broken Dishes pattern, making the block pattern less prominent than the pattern of the actual fabrics. For block-making instructions see page 166.

Swimming Pool Quilt

This large bed quilt is based on palette 38 and is inspired by the way light refracts and reflects on a swimming pool surface. The fabric choices include some very strong curvaceous patterns and so the quilt design counterpoints this with large, simple, angular blocks that repeat diagonally across the quilt.

You Will Need

- ❖ 1½yd wax print fabric in turquoise, blue, and silver
- ❖ 1yd Lizzie House Hello Pilgrim Jewel, Blue
- ❖ 1½yd vintage small white print on sky blue
- ❖ ½yd Lizzie House Constellations Moonphase, Night
- ❖ 54 × 78in batting
- ❖ 54 × 78in backing fabric
- ❖ White quilting thread

Finished quilt size 48½ × 72½in

Further ideas

The quilting I've done here is machined wiggly lines to replicate the way the highlights dance across the rippled surface of a pool. If you were having your quilt long-arm quilted, you could try a more intricate looped pattern for a similar effect, or go in the other direction entirely with angular lines, further adding to the refracted look.

To Make the Quilt

1 Cut the fabrics for the blocks as follows:
- ❖ Pinwheels: 12 × 6⅞in squares of both pale blue and wax print fabrics
- ❖ Four Patch: 12 × 6½in squares of both Jewel and Moonphase fabrics
- ❖ Four Patch Quarter-Square Triangles: 12 × 7¼in squares of both pale blue and wax print fabrics
- ❖ Quarter-Square Triangles: 3 × 13¼in squares of both Jewel and wax print fabrics

2 Make 6 of each of the 4 types of block, referring to chapter 10 for block-making instructions. Ensure that all seams are pressed and measure each main block once it is sewn, trimming to the correct size of 12½in square if necessary.

3 Lay the blocks out and arrange them to form a diagonal stripe pattern as here (see diagram opposite), or other pattern of your choice. When you are happy with the arrangement it's a good idea to take a quick photograph for reference.

4 Starting at the top, sew the blocks together in rows. Press these seams in the same direction on each row, but alternate the direction from row to row so that they nest together in the next step.

5 Sew each row of blocks together, nesting the seams for a neat finish. Press the seams.

6 See page 214 for instructions on how to make up your quilt. Once the quilt "sandwich" is pinned or basted together, thread your machine with quilting cotton and quilt in wavy lines both horizontally and vertically, slicing through the blocks at regular intervals. See page 217 for binding instructions, using the remaining fabrics for the binding.

 Lizzie House Constellations
Moonphase, Night

 Wax print in turquoises,
blue and silver

Lizzie House Hello Pilgrim
Jewel, Blue

Vintage small white print
on sky blue

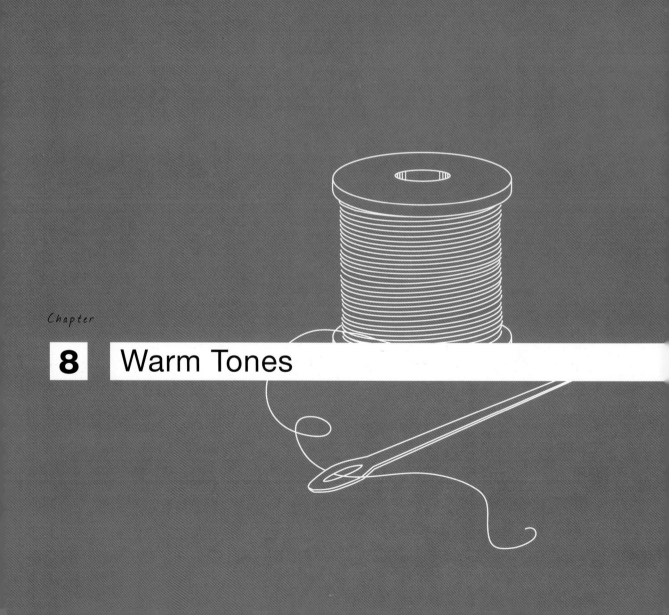

Chapter

8 Warm Tones

Come and bask in the warm colors from the red side of the color wheel (see page 12), which include rosy pinks, reddish purples, olive greens, and teal blues as well as reds—and shades and tones of those colors for light, dark, muted, or vibrant versions. This group of colors tends to have a traditional, classic feel, possibly because so many of the hues are natural and therefore familiar. Warm tones make great quilts for large spaces or for adding a friendly, comforting splash of color to very neutral-colored rooms.

If all the warmth in the palettes here is a little overwhelming, add instant freshness by bringing a solid or subtly textured white into the palette. Remember, too, that when it comes to making a quilt, the binding can alter the overall color balance if you so desire. The Tumbling Blocks quilt at the end of this chapter (see page 140) uses a warm palette of terracotta, pink, and mossy greens with a little cream in the background of the patterned fabrics. It's cosy and traditional—but adding a solid cream binding allows it enough freshness to avoid warm color overload.

41 Royalty

The traditional Chinese prints and textures chosen for this palette all have a rather regal feel due to the purples and golds used. By introducing some cream and paler shades into the patterns the overall look isn't too rich, and they work as a good foil for the deeper shades.

Flying Geese

This block is great for showcasing medium-scale pattern fabrics, showing enough at once to let the pattern be apparent while still retaining a traditional patchwork look. Repeat across a whole quilt or use in borders of a more complex design—Flying Geese combines well with any design made up of squares or right-angled triangles. For block-making instructions see page 174.

Fabric Choices

1 Chinese peacock pattern print cotton

2 Chinese floral pattern print cotton

3 Purple cotton with white blossom print

Ohio Star

A simple star to piece, this block makes good use of the contrast between the plainer purple fabric and the two more colorful ones. As the Quarter-Square Triangle pieces of the star are so small the different fabrics used are indistinct, and so this would be a good choice of block if you had a lot of scraps of similar colored patterned fabrics to use. For block-making instructions see page 197.

Further ideas

A quilt made from fabrics such as these would look great quilted with an intricate floral design, whether by long-arm machine or hand-stitching. Loops and curves will reflect the beautiful swirls in petals and feathers, enhancing the warmth and welcoming feel of the palette.

Six-Sided Star

This block can be left as a hexagon, omitting the four edge triangles (see palette 31, page 97). Remember that if you do "square off" the block like this it will be a rectangle, not a square, because of the dimensions of the inner hexagon. Like Flying Geese, rows of these blocks would make a great edging for a more complex design, so long as the seam angles didn't fight with each other. For block-making instructions see page 198.

42 In the Pink

Although not all shades of pink are "warm," most are, and as it is such an eternally popular color you should have no trouble at all sourcing pink patterned fabrics. Touches of cream here and there together with the flash of green in the Tanya Whelan fabric stop the palette from being too overwhelmingly and cloyingly pink.

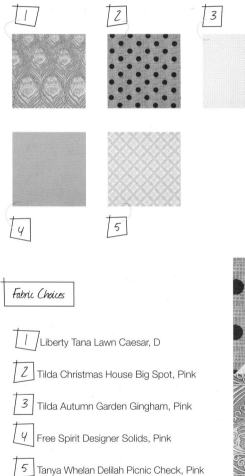

Fabric Choices

1 Liberty Tana Lawn Caesar, D

2 Tilda Christmas House Big Spot, Pink

3 Tilda Autumn Garden Gingham, Pink

4 Free Spirit Designer Solids, Pink

5 Tanya Whelan Delilah Picnic Check, Pink

Churn Dash

Churn Dash brings all five fabrics together in a real riot of pattern. By using the same fabric in all four corners, dotty diamonds would be created if the block were repeated across a quilt, creating a coherent pattern "between" the blocks and balancing the bright check pattern in the central squares. For block-making instructions see page 178.

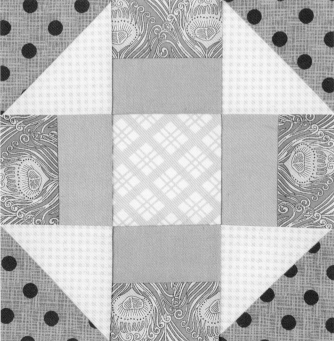

Flower Basket

Making the Flower Basket pattern stand out within the block can be difficult with a palette with only one color, but there is just enough range in tone and pattern within the fabric choices here to make it possible. For a whole quilt, try keeping the solid pink the same across all the blocks but varying the positions of the other fabrics to create more visual interest. For block-making instructions see page 171.

Streak o' Lightning

This version of the Streak o' Lightning block is reasonably subtle for what is usually a very arresting block because of the limited colors. The solid and dotty fabrics are tonally similar, too, so only one of the "streaks"— the paler gingham—stands out. If this were substituted for the Liberty fabric, the effect would be very soft, creating a really gentle look from a graphic block. For block-making instructions see page 189.

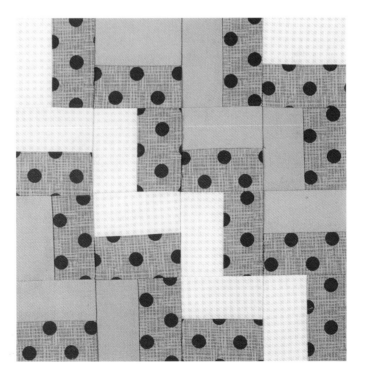

Further ideas

If this palette is just a little too pink for your taste, try adding in a little more green to tie in with the Tanya Whelan fabric, or substitute a solid warm cream for the solid pink fabric to balance things out a little.

43 # Window Box

The combination of warm terracotta with leafy greens always makes me think of window boxes on sills and balconies of city apartments, and the pink flowers in the Liberty fabric here enhance the look. For a full quilt based on this palette and the Tumbling Blocks block, see page 140.

Tumbling Blocks

Although the tonal difference between the green and terracotta fabrics isn't that great, the difference in color allows this block to be a success, creating the three-dimensional look so crucial to it. The block isn't difficult to piece but does rely on accurate cutting and seam allowances in order to create the crisp lines required. For block-making instructions see page 203.

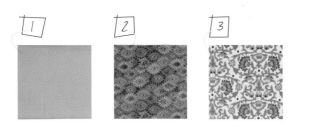

1 Vintage cotton, solid pale terracotta

2 Chinese print cotton in warm green and gray

3 Vintage Liberty Lodden cotton in greens and pinks

Windblown Star

This is a really interesting way of arranging Half-Square Triangles, achieving a relatively complex look with straightforward piecing. The block would work well with any three fabrics that have a decent range of tonal difference. For block-making instructions see page 195.

Attic Windows

This block works well with the fabric choices here as there is enough interest in the Liberty fabric for it to be used in the central square, and the terracotta and green are different enough from each other and tonally different from the Liberty fabric to create the "window" effect. For block-making instructions see page 191.

Further ideas

The terracotta I've used here is a solid, but a textured or patterned terracotta would look great too, adding more interest to the palette. You could even use two or three different fabrics, so long as the colors were similar and the patterns not too loud.

44 Summer Flowers

The hot colors of summer flowers create a vibrancy that is emulated in this palette—warm purples, oranges, reds, and golds with dashes of cooling green and off-white. For a less intense palette try adding in a little more green and some paler tones, either by modifying the fabric choices here or adding in a couple more fabrics.

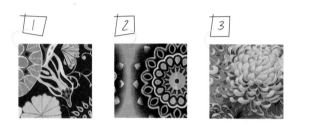

Fabric Choices

1 Valori Wells Cocoon Metamorphosis, Rubywine

2 Wax print in warm purples and peach

3 Philip Jacobs Japanese Chrysanthemum, Green

Robbing Peter to Pay Paul

The pattern created by this block is quite understated here as the two fabrics are tonally very similar, but anchored in different types of purple. However, if you repeated this across a whole quilt, the pattern would become more distinct, creating a drenched-in-color look. For block-making instructions see page 179.

Boxed Square

By framing the warmest patterned fabric with the slightly cooler ones you would be able to create a quilt with regular "hotspots" across it. Rotating the blocks alternately would give a crisscross effect, or keeping them all the same orientation would give a subtle striped look. For block-making instructions see page 186.

Le Moyne Star

This is a great star block to use for fitting in with other blocks, as you can alter the size by small increments by lengthening or shortening the diamond-shaped parallelogram pieces and altering the surrounding squares and right-angled triangles accordingly. By using the fabrics with greatest contrast in the "star" a slight windmill effect is apparent. For block-making instructions see page 193.

Further ideas

This palette creates a real riot of color, and as such will create a very dominating quilt—so proceed with caution! It would be perfect for using outdoors or in an outdoor space such as a summer house or gazebo, or for adding the wow factor to an otherwise neutral-colored room.

45 Folk Art

Deep red and warm white or cream are a great folksy combination, creating an earthy, welcoming look. The fabrics chosen here balance plains and patterns, with patterns kept classic and low-key. A quilt from this palette would fit happily into most surroundings, making it an ideal gift.

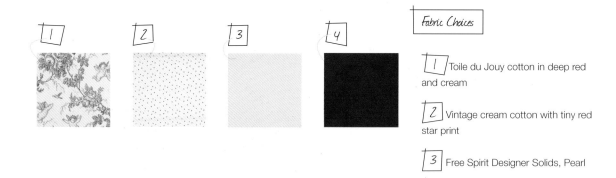

Fabric Choices

1	Toile du Jouy cotton in deep red and cream
2	Vintage cream cotton with tiny red star print
3	Free Spirit Designer Solids, Pearl
4	Riley Blake Shades, Wagon Red

Grandmother's Flower Garden

The traditional nature of this block really suits the palette, and if you attached the hexagons with English paper-piecing, the hand-stitching would add a further folksy feel. You could add extra hexagons to this block to create a larger "flower" or simply appliqué it to foundation fabric to create a focal point to the center of a quilt—or pillow, bag, tablecloth, and so on. For block-making instructions see page 206.

Nine Patch

Another classic block for a classic palette. The lovely checkered effect here again adds to the folksy feel of the fabric choices. I've opted for a diagonal repeat of the different fabrics but they could be placed more randomly to give a scrappy, vintage look. For block-making instructions see page 168.

Further ideas

This palette is one where a little bit of wonky stitching, a wobble in the quilting, or a slight unbalance in the color distribution would only enhance the charming folk-art look.

Melon Patch

Setting the larger toile de Jouy pattern against alternating plains looks great, and all that is needed to finish off the effect is some hand-quilting, especially around the edges of the appliqué pieces. Adding some hand-embroidery would make this block an interesting feature on a quilt, or would create a lovely throw pillow. For block-making instructions see page 208.

46 Falling Leaves

The beautiful natural colors of the Fall are the inspiration behind this palette, with earthy tones of brown and warm green mingling with bright oranges, burgundies and golds. A tiny bit of relief from all of the fiery warmth is given with the sky-blue dots and cream flowers in the Denyse Schmidt fabric, freshening the scheme.

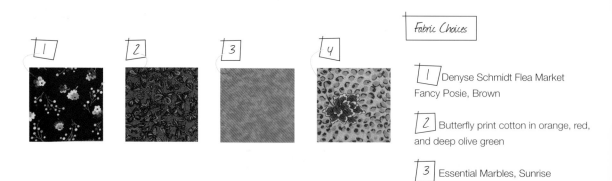

Fabric Choices

1 Denyse Schmidt Flea Market Fancy Posie, Brown

2 Butterfly print cotton in orange, red, and deep olive green

3 Essential Marbles, Sunrise

4 Kaffe Fassett Peking, Rust

Log Cabin

The palette fabrics have a natural tonal split with two deep colors and two mid-tones, so the Log Cabin block works really well with them. I've kept with the traditional pattern but there are many variations of Log Cabin that give a more modern approach, including using "wonky," slightly asymmetrical strips, or creating an off-center block by cutting the strips of one color thinner than the other. For block-making instructions see page 184.

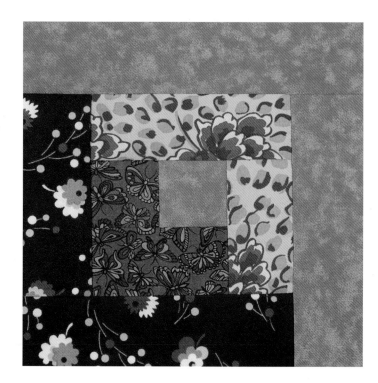

Flying Geese

The Flying Geese triangles remind me of leaf shapes, so it seemed natural to combine this block with the palette. For a real "fallen leaves" look, alternate all of the fabrics within the blocks to create a dappled effect of color and pattern—similar to what you'll see on a walk through the woods in the Fall. For block-making instructions see page 174.

Further ideas

Try other classic blocks with this palette such as Nine Patch (see page 168) or Jacob's Ladder (see page 173). Anything that gives an overall dappled effect will work really well with the theme.

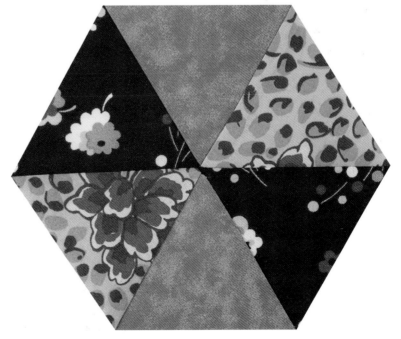

Triangle Hexagon

Unlike the other sample blocks for the palette, this block contrasts the fabrics quite sharply, giving real visual punch. Try combining a group of these at different rotations for varied visual effects, or alternate with plain hexagons of each fabric for quicker results. For block-making instructions see page 202.

Tumbling Blocks Quilt

The Window Box theme of palette 43 (see page 132) is the inspiration behind this quilt, though I have added in more fabrics for variety. The quilting has been done in simple straight lines and mainly in the ditch, but would also look great if it were more of a feature, perhaps in a floral pattern to echo the pale floral fabrics used.

You Will Need

- ❖ 1yd 44in-wide vintage cotton, solid pale terracotta
- ❖ 1yd 44in-wide cotton in shades of warm green and gray.
  I used an assortment of different fabrics
- ❖ ¾yd vintage Liberty Lodden cotton in greens and pinks
- ❖ ¾yd vintage Laura Ashley cotton with tiny pink floral print
- ❖ 46 × 60in batting
- ❖ 46 × 60in backing fabric
- ❖ ½yd Klona Cotton, Cream for the binding
- ❖ Variegated muted green quilting thread

Finished quilt size 40½ × 53½in

Further ideas

I have used relatively large diamonds and machine-piecing for the quilt top, but the vintage nature of many of the fabrics would suit a smaller Tumbling Block with hand-piecing.

To Make the Quilt

1 Cut the fabrics for the blocks as follows:

❖ Terracotta: 40 diamonds with 60-degree angle and equal 5⅛in sides. You should be able to cut 7 from a 44 × 4½in strip of fabric

❖ Greens: proceed as for terracotta. I cut 4½in fabric strips from my variety of greens and pieced the strips together before cutting the diamonds to save fabric

❖ Liberty Lodden: 25 diamonds equal in size to the terracotta and green ones

❖ Laura Ashley floral print: proceed as for Liberty Lodden

2 See page 203 for instructions on how to make Tumbling Blocks, and use either the English paper-piecing method or, as I have done here, the machine-piecing method. Be sure to use accurate seam allowances to preserve all the correct angles.

3 Join your blocks together to build up the quilt top, using the diagram opposite for reference.

4 Trim the edges of the quilt top to create a rectangle. The top should measure around 40 × 53in.

5 See page 214 for instructions on how to make up your quilt. Once the quilt "sandwich" is pinned or basted together, thread your machine with the quilting cotton and quilt in the ditch between the green and terracotta blocks, keeping the line straight as it passes through the lighter "tops" of the blocks and into the next ditch. See page 217 for binding instructions, using the solid cream for the binding. Alternatively, you could use the remaining quilt top fabrics for a scrappier look.

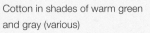 Vintage cotton, solid pale terracotta

 Vintage Liberty Lodden cotton in greens and pinks

Cotton in shades of warm green and gray (various)

Vintage Laura Ashley cotton with tiny pink floral print

Chapter

9  Clear Contrasts

The theme of this chapter is one of contrasts, and the palettes tend toward clean, crisp colors, with some contrasting warm and earthy hues here and there. From starry night skies in palette 47 (see page 146) to patriotic red, white, and blue in palette 52 (see page 156), these are the color combinations that will create eye-catching, graphic quilts with a fresh, modern feel. Block pattern choice, of course, plays into this, and you'll notice a lot of three-dimensional effects in this chapter from the different tonal values of the chosen fabrics.

Contrasts don't have to lie simply with careful choice of colors and block pattern. You can achieve wonderful contrasts with fabric pattern, too, either by counter-pointing small-scale and large-scale patterns (see palette 48, page 148, and the quilt based on it at the end of the chapter, page 158), or by putting curves with lines, dots with checks, geometrics with florals (see Chapter 2 for more about pattern contrasts).

Quilting style can add further textural contrast to a quilt. The quilt at the end of Chapter 6 is a good example of how the linear, angular nature of a Log Cabin block can be contrasted with the concentric circles created by the quilting texture.

47 Cosmic

The colors of the cosmos form one of the best contrasts mother nature has to offer—bright bluish stars against a dark sky, almost black and white but with a subtle infusion of color. The fabrics for the palette here already explore the theme, plus I've added a solid ice blue to balance the tones a little.

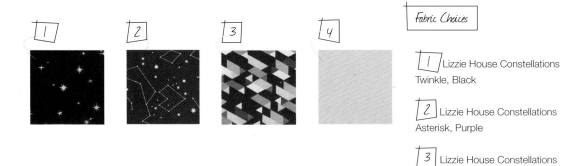

Fabric Choices

1 Lizzie House Constellations Twinkle, Black

2 Lizzie House Constellations Asterisk, Purple

3 Lizzie House Constellations Supernova, Purple

4 Free Spirit Designer Solids, Ice

Triangle Hexagon

The angles in this block look great with the angular Supernova fabric, giving even more crispness to the already clean and sharp palette. You could further enhance this effect with the quilting, using angular lines and even adding in star shapes or starburst effects with white or pale-blue quilting thread. For block-making instructions see page 202.

Inner City

Inner City is a tessellating hexagon pattern that gives a really interesting three-dimensional effect when repeated across a whole quilt top. It is relatively simple to piece, either by machine or using English paper-piecing, and works best with a light, mid-tone and dark fabric, as here. For block-making instructions see page 204.

Attic Windows

This is an interesting treatment of Attic Windows, with two of the patterned fabrics framing the solid ice blue to give a very strong, graphic look. Repeat this block as it is to get a great three-dimensional effect, or soften the look by varying the fabric positions within the blocks. For block-making instructions see page 191.

Further ideas

If you like the colors here but not the cosmic theme, try mixing black and white fabrics with a pastel or mid-tone color for a retro fifties look. Solids would work well for this but small patterns would be great too.

48 Olives by the Pool

Bright turquoise and olive green offer a great contrast of warm and cool colors, and with some deep navy and cream in the mix the overall palette gains tonal variety too. All of the palette fabrics here are by Amy Butler, two from the same collection, so the colors have already been chosen by the fabric designer to work well together.

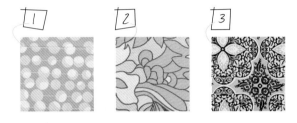

Robbing Peter to Pay Paul

This block is usually made using just two fabrics but here all three from the palette have been included to give an interesting effect. You could carry on with this logic across a whole quilt, varying the positions of the three fabrics to enhance visual interest. For block-making instructions see page 179.

Fabric Choices

1 Amy Butler Midwest Modern Martini, Moss

2 Amy Butler Daisy Chain Wildflowers, Turquoise

3 Amy Butler Daisy Chain Pressed Flowers, Turquoise

Boxed Square

This block allows the large-scale pattern of the Wildflowers fabric to be shown in the large rectangular shapes, with the smaller-scale fabrics inhabiting the squares. It could be mixed really successfully with any block based on the Nine-Patch geometry, or would look great used alone with alternate blocks rotated for a woven look. For block-making instructions see page 186.

Further ideas

The different pattern scales used in this palette add to the contrast between the fabrics, but with large-scale patterns it is a good idea to allow them to be used in relatively large pieces in at least some of the blocks of a quilt, so bear this in mind when choosing blocks.

Basket Weave

As with Robbing Peter to Pay Paul, this block is more often made with just two fabrics, but here using all three adds more variety to the pattern scales and colors. There are lots of quilt design possibilities with these blocks, either by rotating some of the blocks to create different graphic effects, or by varying the positions of the fabrics. You could even try a mixture of both, but be careful your design doesn't get "lost" in the mix! For block-making instructions see page 187.

49 Citrus Burst

The colors of citrus fruits have a natural zing to them, and despite being tonally similar all seem to contrast with each other really well. Pink grapefruit, fresh lemon, luscious lime, and bright orange all work together with a touch of white and simple, modern patterns in this palette to create a really refreshing look.

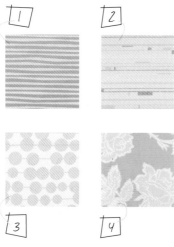

Dutchman's Puzzle

This dynamic block comprises four carefully arranged Flying Geese units, in this case with the large triangles in the same fabric but the smaller "background" triangles in two different fabrics. The directional effect works really well with the citrus brights, making a block that really pops! For block-making instructions see page 175.

Fabric Choices

1 Michelle Engel Bencsko Simpatico Straws, Peachy

2 Heather Bailey Welcome Road, Lemongrass

3 Amy Butler Midwest Modern Martini, Tangerine

4 Heather Bailey Pop Garden Roses 5, Green

Windmill Star

By choosing just three of the fabrics here the graphic effect of the block is shown really well, with the oranges and yellows of the star fabrics standing out against the slightly darker green pattern. You could alternate the colors in the star points for a different effect. For block-making instructions see page 194.

Brick Wall

The arrangement of fabrics in this block, made up of 25 squares, is what gives it its name, and the central diagonal in orange looks great against the surrounding greens and yellows. Both of the stripe fabrics have been sewn so that the stripes are in the same direction, but you could rotate alternate squares for even more impact. For block-making instructions see page 165.

Further ideas

This palette would look great with a range of solids in citrus colors, as there is so much contrast in the colors of the palette it doesn't really need pattern. Using a couple of different shades of each citrus color would add further interest and allow lots of design scope.

50 Valentine

Red and off-white features in palette 45 (see page 136), and it's interesting to see the very different effect here using brighter red, pure white, and bold, graphic patterns. You could easily introduce solid red and white to the palette, and further patterned fabrics, so long as the patterns remained geometric to preserve the contrasting, modern feel.

Fabric Choices

1 | Striped cotton in red and white

2 | Riley Blake Small Chevron, Red

3 | Tanya Whelan Delilah Dots, Red

Kaleidoscope

This block may have looked a little too hypnotic with all three fabrics included, and so just two have been used. Note that the stripe fabric has been very carefully cut so that the stripes radiate outwards, enhancing the pattern created by the block. For block-making instructions see page 196.

Friendship Star

It's the combination of stripes and spots that creates the contrast here, allowing the star pattern to emerge from the block. The stripe corner squares have been rotated in opposite corners to follow the outline of the star triangles, which works really well. For block-making instructions see page 199.

Further ideas

Getting the quilting to work with such bold patterns could present a challenge. You could play it safe with in-the-ditch stitching, or go for bold, straight lines that follow the angles of some of the block seams.

Jacob's Ladder

Bringing in the chevron stripe fabric lets the block pattern take shape here. You could create a wonderfully bright and graphic yet simple quilt with these blocks. Either repeat the fabric positions as here and play around with rotating some of the blocks, or vary the fabric positions to add extra interest. A symmetrical placement of blocks across the quilt top would probably work best with these geometric patterns. For block-making instructions see page 173.

51 | Meadow

Sky blue, sunny yellow, and grass green always look great together, but scatter a handful of meadow flower colors in and you have a palette bursting with happy, summer contrasts. The fabric choices here are quite a jumble of different styles, but this works with the theme as an assortment of texture and color that feels quite natural.

Crazy Patchwork

This is a perfect block for such a mishmash of a palette, creating a slightly chaotic look that nonetheless hangs together well. You could combine crazy blocks for a quilt top, or keep adding to the block to create a whole quilt top from one huge Crazy Patchwork block. For block-making instructions see page 213.

Fabric Choices

1 Free Spirit Designer Solids, Yellow

2 Free Spirit Designer Solids, Sky

3 Carolyn Friedlander Architextures Contours, Green

4 Denyse Schmidt Flea Market Fancy Medallion, Green

5 IKEA Helle Vilén

Trailing Star

Here, the solid yellow is given
prominence as the background fabric,
with the patterned "trails" of the star
receding slightly in the block.
A Trailing Star quilt with fabrics
alternating across the blocks would
make a wonderfully cheerful quilt,
perfect for a child's room. For block-
making instructions see page 192.

Further ideas

If you wanted to make a really quick quilt,
try sewing simple 8in squares of the
patterned fabrics together to create a quilt
top of the required size. Make up the quilt
using straightforward ditch quilting and then
use the solid blue and yellow in the binding.

Flower Basket

With such a riot of color going on a
Flower Basket block is a natural choice.
Just four of the five fabrics have been
used here, so that the "flowers" part
of the block creates a very strong
and graphic look. The basket part
of the block merges a little with
the background, but if you want
a stronger contrast, simply replace
one of the green patterned fabrics with
the solid yellow. For block-making
instructions see page 171.

52 Patriotic

Red, white, and blue are used on the flags of many countries, and you can see why. They provide great contrast, so can be seen from a distance, and they bring together the two strongest primary colors with the ultimate contrast shade—white. Here, a heritage feel has been brought to the palette by using very slightly toned down versions of each color.

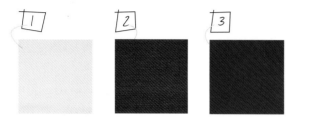

Fabric Choices

1 Vintage white linen

2 Kaffe Fassett Shot Cotton, Scarlet

3 Free Spirit Designer Solids, Yale Blue

Indian Arrowhead

It may not look it but this lovely block is one of the most difficult to piece accurately, so it's not for the faint-hearted. The effect of the contrasting solid fabrics is fabulous, however, so it's worth persevering with to add one or more focal points to your quilt. For block-making instructions see page 212.

Tumbling Blocks

The palette fabrics are ideal for the three-dimensional effect of Tumbling Blocks. While a whole quilt of Tumbling Blocks in solid fabrics may look a little dull, you could always add some interesting texture on top with the quilting, using an intricate swirling pattern for contrast, or even some Sashiko style hand-quilting (see page 46). For block-making instructions see page 203.

Further ideas

This palette would work equally well with patterned or textured fabrics, so long as the strict scheme of red, white, and blue were adhered to. Small-scale, textural patterns rather than large, pictorial ones would work best.

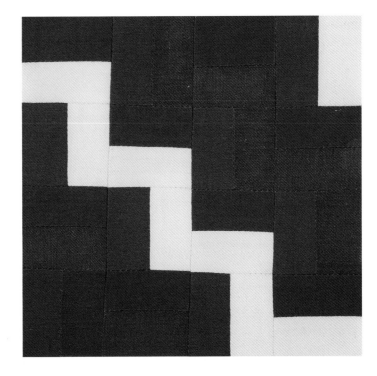

Streak o' Lightning

Solid contrasting colors are probably the best way to make this block live up to its name, especially when one of the streaks is white! As with Tumbling Blocks, a whole quilt made of this block in solid colors could be a little dull, but you could add interesting quilting following the lines of the streaks, perhaps using red or blue thread on the white streak. For block-making instructions see page 189.

Big Chevrons Quilt

This small bed quilt is based on palette 48 (see page 148), which includes a particularly large-scale fabric pattern. I've therefore opted for a scaled-up version of Chevrons, separated by long lines of sashing for a more graphic effect. You could, of course, scale the Chevrons back down again, but bear in mind more fabric will be needed for more seam allowances.

You Will Need

❖ 1¼yd Amy Butler Midwest Modern Martini, Moss

❖ 1¼yd Amy Butler Daisy Chain Wildflowers, Turquoise

❖ 1yd Amy Butler Daisy Chain Pressed Flowers, Turquoise

❖ ½yd 44in-wide solid turquoise cotton for binding

❖ 54 × 78in batting

❖ 54 × 78in backing fabric

❖ Olive green quilting thread

Finished quilt size 48 × 72in

Further ideas

Try adding more fabrics into the Chevrons for extra interest—choosing fabrics from the same range will ensure good color combinations but you should be able to match in other designs reasonably easily. Just keep the diamonds in a regular alternating pattern and it's bound to look good!

To Make the Quilt

1. Cut the fabrics for the blocks as follows:
- ❖ Martini: 8 strips across the width of the fabric, each measuring 4¾in high
- ❖ Wildflowers: 8 strips across the width of the fabric, each measuring 4¾in high
- ❖ Pressed Flowers: 8 strips across the width of the fabric, each measuring 3½in high

2. The most efficient way to make the Chevron strips is with strip-piecing, staggering the strips in order to avoid too much fabric wastage. This is best done in blocks for ease of sewing and cutting. Take 2 strips of Martini and 2 strips of Wildflower, and lay them long sides together, alternating the fabrics. Using a quilter's ruler, stagger the ends so that the strips follow a 45-degree angle. Mark positions lightly in pencil and then sew the strips together in this staggered way using accurate ¼in seams.

3. Once you have a block of 4 strips sewn, use your quilter's ruler to cut diagonal strips from the block at a 45-degree angle, keeping to an accurate 6½in between each cut. You should have 5 strips of 4 diamond shapes.

4. Repeat steps 2 and 3 once more, staggering the strips of Martini and Wildflower in the same direction as before. Repeat steps 2 and 3 twice more, but staggering the strips of Martini and Wildflower in the OPPOSITE direction, and cutting in the opposite direction too.

5. Sew the diamond strips together to create 3 strips of 14 diamonds in one direction, and 3 strips of 14 diamonds in the other direction. This will involve a little seam unpicking of the strips to get to 14.

6. Pair up the joined strips to get the Chevron effect, matching the fabrics at the joins. You have an extra diamond on each strip to allow this to happen easily, so your ends probably won't be the same height. As long as 13 of the 14 diamonds are sewn together, all is well. Sew together, matching seams carefully.

7. Join the 3 Chevron strips together with the sashing strips and press the quilt top carefully. Trim the top and bottom of the quilt top to form straight lines.

8. See page 214 for instructions on how to make up your quilt. Once the quilt "sandwich" is pinned or basted together, thread your machine with the quilting cotton and quilt in the ditch between the stripes. See page 217 for binding instructions, using the solid turquoise fabric for the binding.

 Amy Butler Midwest Modern Martini, Moss

Amy Butler Daisy Chain Pressed Flowers, Turquoise

 Amy Butler Daisy Chain Wildflowers, Turquoise

 Solid turquoise cotton for binding

10 Putting it All Together

Here, you will find all the technical details for how to put together the quilt blocks featured throughout this book. As quilt blocks can be made to more or less any size you require, measurements have not been given in most cases. Simply use the instructions to see how the blocks fit together, and decide on the size you would like to make. Remember to add a ¼in seam allowance around each separate piece of fabric.

At the end of the chapter there are step-by-step instructions on how to construct a basic quilt, including how to quilt, trim, and bind it for professional results. However, there are many other ways to create a quilt that go beyond the scope of these pages, so have a look on the internet, ask at your local fabric store, talk to fellow quilters, and find the methods that suit you best.

Although the emphasis in this book is on the creative aspect of putting colors, patterns, and textures together for fabulous quilts, bear in mind that quilt-making is a precise art. Ensure that your fabrics are cut accurately and that your seam allowances are correct and consistent, and you'll have stunning quilts.

Four Patch

Apart from a single piece of fabric, a Four-Patch block is one of the simplest to make. You will need four squares in two different colors (usually light and dark). Four-Patch blocks can also be created by strip-piecing—see below. Use a ¼in seam allowance.

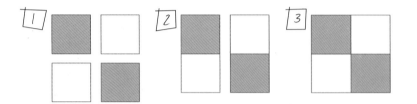

1 Lay out the 4 equal-sized squares in an alternating pattern as shown.

2 Sew the squares together in pairs, pressing the seam toward the darker fabric of each pair.

3 Now sew the pairs together, matching and nesting seams carefully at the center. Press the finished block.

Strip-Pieced Four Patch

Strip-piecing is a quick method to use if you have lots of Four-Patch blocks to create. You will need two long strips of fabric in two different colors or tones.

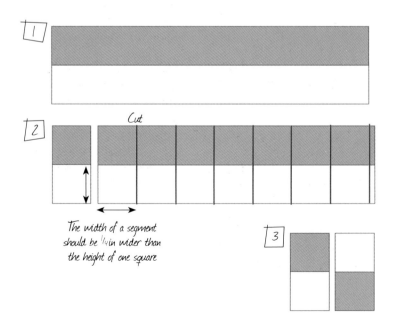

Cut

The width of a segment should be ¼in wider than the height of one square

1 Sew the 2 strips together and press the seam toward the darker fabric.

2 Cut the combined strip into segments, with the width of the segments equal to the height of a single square plus ¼in seam allowance.

3 Take pairs of units and rotate 1. Sew them together, matching seams carefully at the center. Press each block.

Brick Wall

For this straightforward block you will need 25 squares of fabric. For the block shown choose five dark squares, nine medium squares, nine light squares and two contrast-color squares. You can create different visual effects by varying the color combinations or the block orientation. Use a ¼in seam allowance.

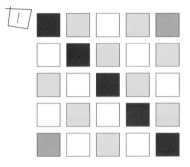

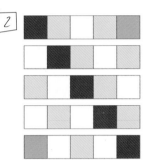

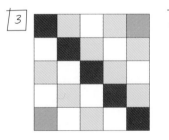

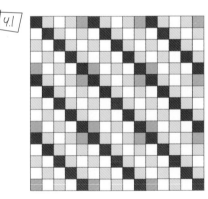

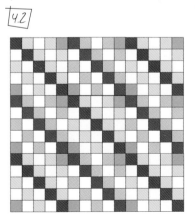

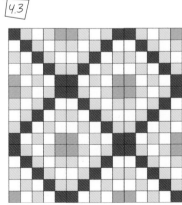

1 Lay out your squares in the pattern shown.

2 Sew the squares together in rows, so that you have 5 rows. Press the seams in the same direction on each row, but alternate the direction from row to row. So, for the top row press to the left, the next row down to the right, the next row down to the left again, and so on. That way, your seams will nest when sewing the rows together.

3 Sew the rows together, taking care to align the seam junctions neatly. Press the row seams all in the same direction, and, if making multiple blocks, alternate the direction between blocks to ensure seams nest when blocks are sewn together.

4 The Brick Wall block is an easy one to repeat, creating a design with a strong diagonal movement (4.1). Changing the color combinations for some of the blocks can bring more life to the design (4.2), or try rotating alternate blocks for a lattice effect (4.3).

Half-Square Triangle

Half-Square Triangle blocks are very popular and often form smaller units in larger blocks. You will need two squares in two different colors or patterns (usually light and dark). Use a ¼in seam allowance.

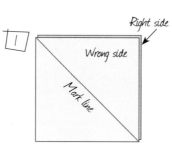

|1| Mark a diagonal line on the back of 1 square. Place the squares right sides together, matching edges exactly.

|2| Pin the squares together and sew ¼in either side of the marked diagonal line. These lines can be marked, or use the ¼in foot on your machine to guide you.

|3| Cut the 2 triangles apart on the diagonal line.

|4| You will have 2 identical units. Press the units, usually with the seam toward the darker fabric.

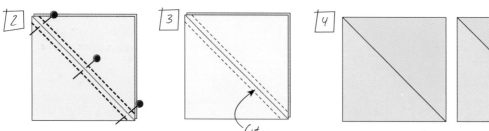

Broken Dishes

This is one of the most popular patchwork blocks. It's easy to make and works well with many other blocks to create interesting patterns. All you need are four Half-Square Triangle units (see above). Use a ¼in seam allowance.

|1| Make four Half-Square Triangle units. Lay the completed Half-Square Triangle units out as shown.

|2| Sew the units together in pairs, alternating the colors and with the diagonal lines running in the correct direction. Keep an accurate ¼in seam allowance.

|3| Finally, sew the 2 halves of the block together, aligning the center seam carefully, as well as the edge triangle seams.

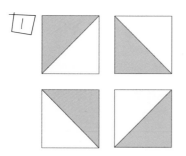

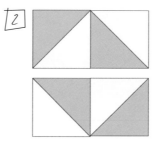

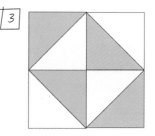

Quarter-Square Triangle

Quarter-Square Triangle blocks can be made in a similar way to Half-Square Triangles (see opposite). The quarter triangles can all be different colors but the instructions here show just two. You will need two squares in two different colors. Use a ¼in seam allowance.

1 | Begin by making 2 Half-Square Triangle units.

2 | Pin the 2 units right sides together, exactly one on top of the other, with their diagonal lines going in the same direction and with the colors opposite each other. Mark a diagonal line perpendicular to the seam across the top square. Sew ¼in either side of the marked line.

3 | Cut the 2 units apart on the marked diagonal line.

4 | You will have 2 identical units. Press the units open, usually toward the darker fabric.

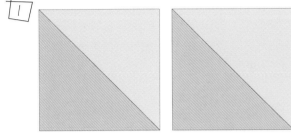

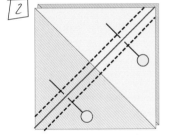

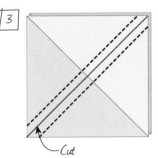

Cut

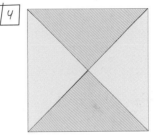

Pinwheel

Pinwheels are made from four squares, each square containing two right-angled triangles. (Follow the method on page 166 to create the Half-Square Triangles used in this block.) Use a ¼in seam allowance.

1 Make 4 Half-Square Triangle units, then arrange the units as shown. Sew the units together in pairs and then sew the 2 halves of the block together.

2 Press the finished block. The pinwheel effect will be more apparent if contrasting colors or tones are used, as shown.

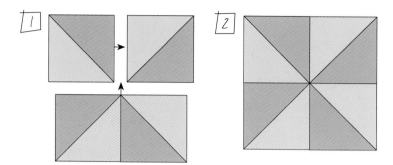

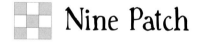

Nine Patch

A Nine-Patch block is used in many patchwork patterns. It can be created with separate squares or by strip-piecing in a similar way to a Four-Patch block. You will need nine squares in total. These can all be different or a light and dark combination. Use a ¼in seam allowance.

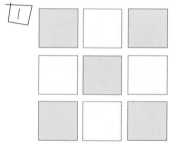

1 Arrange the squares in the pattern you wish, or alternating light and dark as here.

2 Sew the squares together in rows. The rows can be horizontal or vertical. Press the seams in the top and bottom rows in the same direction and the seams in the middle row in the opposite direction. This will help the seams nest together neatly when the rows are joined.

3 Sew the rows together, matching seam junctions carefully. Press the finished block.

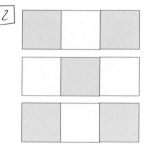

Strip-Pieced Nine Patch

Nine-Patch blocks can be created more quickly by strip-piecing. The method is described in the Four-Patch block instructions on page 164—just use three strips instead of two.

Shoo Fly

This is a popular Nine-Patch block and is relatively fast and simple to make. For a two-color version, as shown here, you will need four squares in one color, one square in a different color, and four Half-Square Triangles (see page 166) made up of the two colors. Use a ¼in seam allowance.

1 / Make 4 Half-Square Triangle units.

2 / Cut your whole squares the same size as the finished Half-Square Triangle units. Arrange the 9 units into the pattern shown.

3 / Sew the units together in rows, pressing the joining seams in one direction for the top and bottom rows and in the opposite direction on the middle row.

4 / Sew the rows together, matching and nesting the seam junctions carefully. Press the finished block.

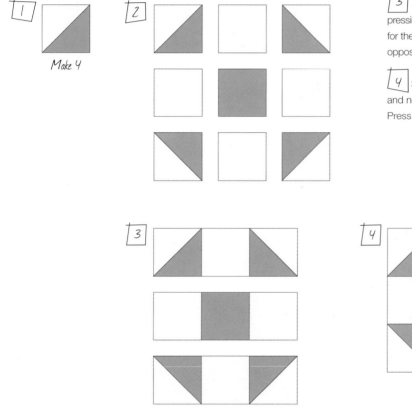

Make 4

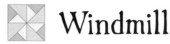 # Windmill

This eye-catching block is made using a combination of Half-Square Triangle units (see page 166) and fabric squares. Your fabric choices will determine the optical effect created here, and you can play around with stripes and swirls to create eye-popping designs. Use a ¼in seam allowance.

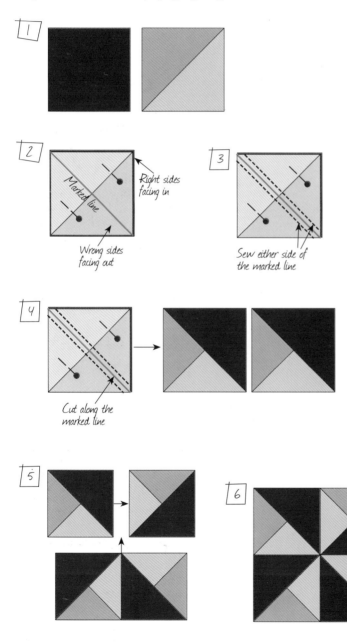

1 Make 2 Half-Square Triangle units. Take a square of fabric and a Half-Square Triangle unit. They must be the same size.

2 Place them right sides together, then mark a diagonal line from corner to corner that is in the opposite direction to the seam in the Half-Square Triangle block. Pin the fabrics together.

3 Sew a seam ¼in either side of the marked line.

4 Cut along the marked line and press each unit open.

5 Repeat steps 1–4. Arrange the 4 units as shown. Sew the units together in pairs.

6 Sew the 2 halves of the block together. The effect will be more apparent if the colors in the larger triangles are different from those in the smaller triangles.

Flower Basket

There are many, many basket designs in patchwork and this 16-patch version is a good example. You will need five squares in one color for the background, one square in a different color for the basket, and ten Half-Square Triangle units made up of five color combinations. (See page 166 for making Half-Square Triangles.) Use a ¼in seam allowance.

1 Make 10 Half-Square Triangle units.

2 Lay out the whole squares and the Half-Square Triangle units in the arrangement shown, taking care to place the Half-Square Triangles in the correct positions and orientations.

3 Sew the units together in rows, pressing the seams of the first and third rows in one direction and the seams of the second and fourth rows in the other direction.

4 Now sew the rows together, aligning and nesting the seams carefully. Press the block.

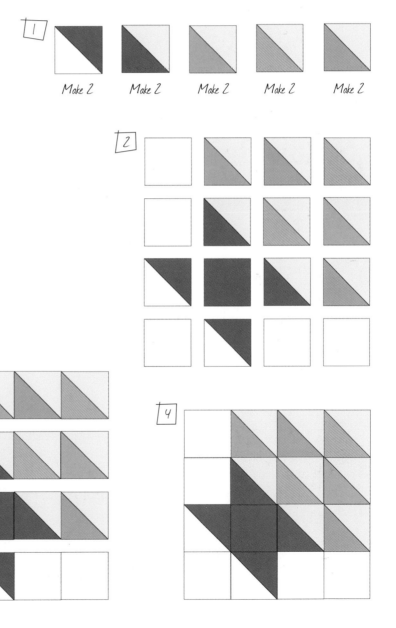

Make 2   Make 2   Make 2   Make 2   Make 2

Card Trick

This block pattern looks complicated but is actually very simple to construct—so long as you cut accurately and use a consistent ¼in seam allowance. (See page 166 for making Half-Square Triangles and page 167 for making Quarter-Square Triangles.)

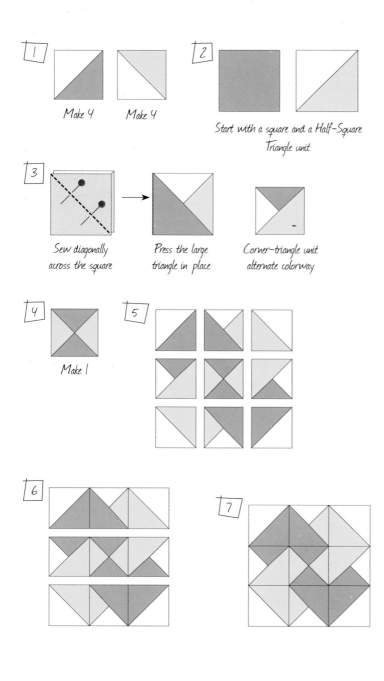

1 | Make 4 Make 4

2 | Start with a square and a Half-Square Triangle unit

3 | Sew diagonally across the square Press the large triangle in place Corner-triangle unit alternate colorway

4 | Make 1

5 |

6 |

7 |

1 | First make your Half-Square Triangle units—4 in pale/dark colors and 4 in pale/medium colors. Put 2 of each colorway aside for the block corners. The remaining 2 of each colorway will be used to make the corner-triangle units in the next step.

2 | The corner-triangle units are made up of a Half-Square Triangle with a larger triangle across one half. Take 1 of your Half-Square Triangle units and a plain square of the fabric not used in the Half-Square Triangle.

3 | Place the square right side down on the Half-Square Triangle unit (right side up), aligning the corners. Draw a diagonal line through the square and then pin the square and the unit together, ensuring that the drawn line is at 90 degrees to the seam of the unit underneath. Sew along the line. Flip the square over, along the stitched line, and press. Trim excess fabric at the back. Make 1 more unit like this, and a further 2 in the alternate colorway.

4 | Make the Quarter-Square Triangle unit for the center of the block (see page 167).

5 | Lay out the units as shown, taking care to place the units in the correct positions and orientations.

6 | Sew the units together in rows, pressing the seams of the top and bottom rows in one direction and the seams of the middle row in the other direction.

7 | Now sew the rows together, aligning the seams carefully.

Jacob's Ladder

There are many versions of this quilt block, but this 16-patch version is straightforward to piece and gives scope for some interesting color combinations. For the pattern shown here you will need six pale squares, four dark squares, two contrast-color squares and four Half-Square Triangle units made up of the pale color and the contrast color. (See page 166 for making Half-Square Triangles.) Use a ¼in seam allowance.

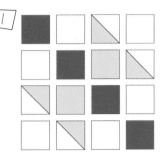

1 Make the 4 Half-Square Triangle units from the pale color and the contrast color. Lay out the units in the arrangement shown, taking care to place the Half-Square Triangle units in the correct orientations.

2 Sew the units together in rows, pressing the seams of the first and third rows in one direction and the seams of the second and fourth rows in the other direction.

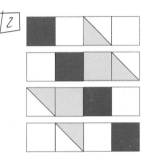

3 Now sew the rows together, aligning and nesting all the seams carefully.

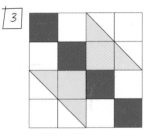

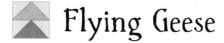 # Flying Geese

The method shown here makes a single Flying Geese unit. You will need one rectangle in one color and two squares in another color. When the block is finished, the smaller squares need to overlap at the center top to allow for a seam allowance, so the rectangle needs to be ½in smaller in length than the combined squares. For example, a 4½in × 2½in rectangle and two 2½in squares would work well. See also Dutchman's Puzzle (opposite) for a block using Flying Geese units. Use a ¼in seam allowance.

1 Place a small square right side down on the rectangle (right side up), aligning the left-hand corners. Draw or crease a diagonal line through the square and pin together. Sew along the line. Fold the bottom corner up to meet the top, and press. Trim the excess fabric from the corner now sitting at the back.

2 Sew the second square to the rectangle in the same way in the opposite corner. Once sewn and pressed, this square will overlap the one already sewn in place.

3 You can make more Flying Geese units and join them together for blocks or borders, as shown.

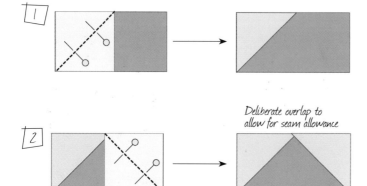

Deliberate overlap to allow for seam allowance

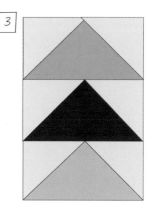

Dutchman's Puzzle

This block is made up of eight Flying Geese units (see opposite), sewn into pairs, with each rotated 90 degrees to form the block pattern. You will need four rectangles in a dark color, four rectangles in a medium color, and 16 squares in a pale color. When the block is finished, the smaller squares need to overlap at the center to allow for a seam allowance, so the rectangle needs to be ½in smaller in length than the combined squares. Use a ¼in seam allowance.

1 Make 8 Flying Geese blocks, 4 with the darker color and 4 with the lighter color, following the instructions on the page opposite.

2 Sew a dark and a light unit together and press.

3 Sew the other 3 pairs together and arrange the pairs, rotating them as shown.

4 Sew 2 pairs together and press the center seams so they lie in opposite directions.

5 Sew the rows together. Press the finished block.

1

Make 4   Make 4

2

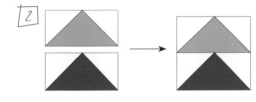

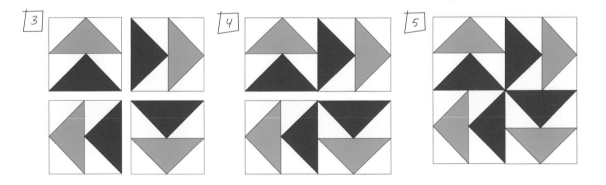

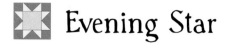 # Evening Star

This easy star block has many names, including Eight-Point Star, Nameless Star and Sawtooth. It is straightforward to make and ideal for playing with color combinations. You could also add different elements to the block, such as a square on point in the center. For the block shown you will need one large central square, four smaller corner squares, and four Flying Geese units (see page 174). Use a ¼in seam allowance.

1 Make 4 Flying Geese units.

2 Sew a Flying Geese unit to each side of the large square, making sure you have the star points going in the right direction. Press seams inward.

3 Sew a small square to each side of the remaining Flying Geese units. Press seams outward.

4 Arrange the block in rows as shown.

5 Sew the rows together. Press the finished block.

Make 4

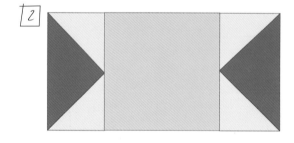

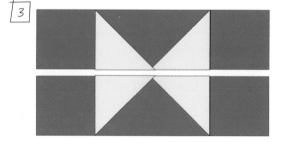

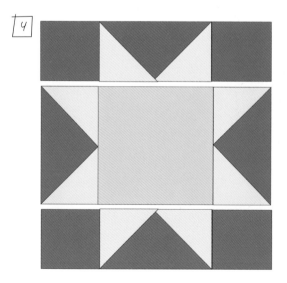

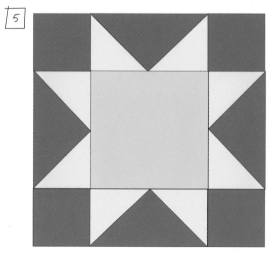

 # Art Square

Also called Village Square, this block creates an attractive regular pattern, often seen in English Victorian tiled floors, when used with a limited color palette. It takes on a different character when combined with a multicolored palette, giving a more scrappy look. You will need one large square for the block center, four small squares, and four Flying Geese units (see page 174). Use a ¼in seam allowance.

Make 4

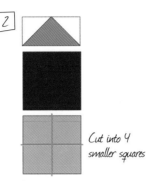

Cut into 4
smaller squares

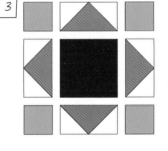

 Make 4 Flying Geese units.

2 Cut a large central square the same length as a Flying Geese unit. Cut a second large square in a different color fabric and cut this in half across the length and width to make 4 smaller squares.

3 Lay out the units for the block as shown.

4 Sew the units together in rows.

5 Sew the rows together. Press the finished block.

6 When sewing multiple blocks together, take care to align seams carefully for a professional finish.

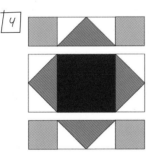

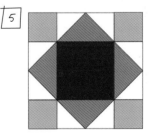

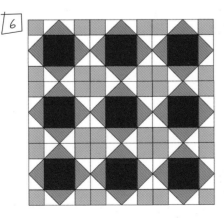

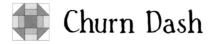

Churn Dash

This quilt block dates back over a century and there are many versions of it. For the pattern shown here you need one square, four Half-Square Triangle units, and four paired rectangles. (See page 166 for making Half-Square Triangles.) Use a ¼in seam allowance.

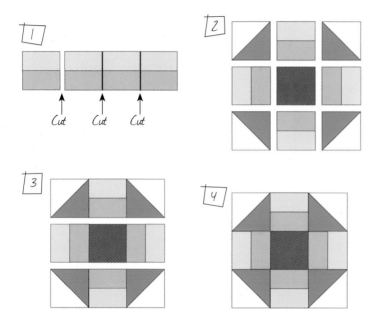

1. Make the paired rectangles. Work out the size you would like each square in the block to be, multiply by 4 plus ½in seam allowance for the length, and divide by 2 plus ½in seam allowance for the width, then cut a strip of these dimensions from 2 different colors and sew them together as shown. Cut the pieced strip into square segments.

2. Make 4 Half-Square Triangle units from 2 contrasting fabrics. Lay out the central square, the Half-Square Triangle units, and the paired rectangles in the arrangement shown.

3. Sew the units together in rows, pressing the seams of the first and last rows in one direction and the seams of the center row in the other direction.

4. Now sew the rows together, aligning and nesting the center seams carefully. Press the finished block.

Bow Tie

There are various ways to make a Bow Tie block. The method shown here is very quick and simple. You will need four large squares in two different colors (preferably a light and a dark for good tonal contrast) and two small squares matching the dark-colored large squares. Use a ¼in seam allowance.

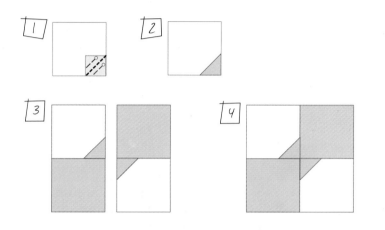

|1| Mark a diagonal line on the wrong side of a small dark square. Place a large light square right side up and the small square on top of it right side down, with corner edges aligned and the marked line in the direction shown. Pin in place and then sew across the diagonal of the small square.

|2| Fold the triangle into place and press. Trim off the excess fabric at the back, leaving a ¼in seam allowance. Make 1 more unit like this so that you have 2.

|3| Lay out the block as shown and sew each pair of units together.

|4| Join the 2 halves of the block. Press the finished block.

Robbing Peter to Pay Paul

This is similar in construction to a Bow Tie block but with small triangles in two corners of all four squares. You will need four large squares in two different colors, and four small squares in each of the two colors of the larger squares.

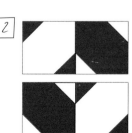

Make 2   Make 2

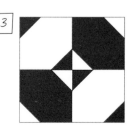

|1| Follow steps 1–2 of Bow Tie above, then add another small square to the corner diagonally opposite. Make 2 units in each colorway.

|2| Lay out the units in the pattern shown, rotating them as needed. Sew the units into pairs.

|3| Join the pairs to finish the block, pressing central seams in opposite directions so that they nest neatly in the center.

 # Snowball

For this block you will need one large square in one color and four small squares in a second color. The block can also be constructed from Half-Square Triangles and whole squares (see below). Use a ¼in seam allowance.

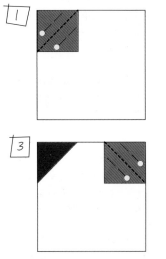

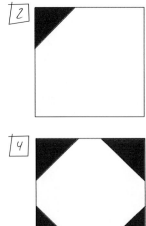

1 Mark a diagonal line on the wrong side of a small dark square. Place the large square right side up and the small square on top, right side down, with corner edges aligned and the marked line in the direction shown. Pin in place. Sew across the diagonal of the small square.

2 Fold the triangle back into place and press. Trim off the excess fabric at the back.

3 Repeat with the other 3 small squares, aligning with the other corners of the large square, sewing the diagonal seam, and pressing the triangles into place.

4 Press the finished block.

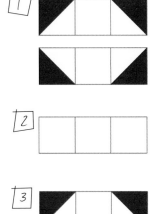

Snowball with Half-Square Triangles

1 You will need 5 small squares and 4 Half-Square Triangle units. See page 166 for making Half-Square Triangles. Sew a Half-Square Triangle unit to each side of a square and press. Repeat to make another row, and rotate 180 degrees before pressing in the same direction as the first row.

2 Sew 3 squares together for the central row. Press these seams in the opposite direction to the top and bottom rows.

3 Sew the 3 rows together with the row of squares in the middle, aligning and nesting the seams carefully. Press the finished block.

 # Octagon

This block can look very similar to Snowball (see opposite) but for a true octagon, each side must be the same measurement. For a finished 6in block you will need one 6in square and four smaller squares each measuring 1¾in (this includes the ¼in seam allowance).

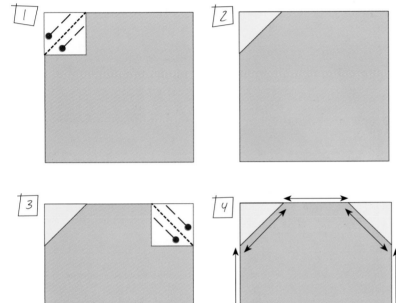

For a true octagon these measurements
must be the same

1 Mark a diagonal line on the wrong side of a small square. Place the large square right side up and the small square on top, right side down, with corner edges aligned and the marked line in the direction shown. Pin in place. Sew across the diagonal of the small square.

2 Fold the triangle into place and press. Trim off the excess fabric at the back.

3 Repeat with the second small square, aligning it with the other corner of the large square, and sew the diagonal seam. Press the triangle into place.

4 Add the other 2 small squares in the same way. Check that the finished block is square, trimming it if necessary.

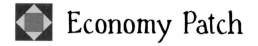 # Economy Patch

The instructions and diagrams here show this block with three colors but it could easily be multicolored, allowing you to use up fabric scraps. The sizes given in the steps will produce a block 5½in square. You will need one 3in square for the block center, two 2½in squares cut along the diagonal to give four triangles for the first round, and two 3¼in squares cut along the diagonal to give four triangles for the second round. Use a ¼in seam allowance.

1 Prepare the pieces for the block.

2 Take 2 small triangles and, with right sides together, sew them to opposite sides of the central square, using ¼in seams. Note that the corners of the triangle will extend past the edges of the square. Press seams outward.

3 Sew the other 2 triangles to the other sides of the square and press. Trim the block square (4in), ensuring the ¼in seam allowance is even all around, ready for the next step.

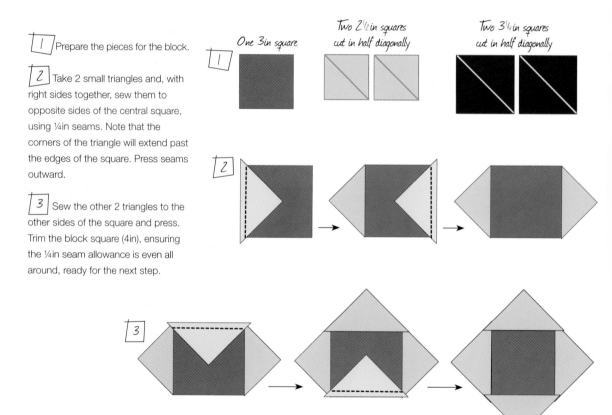

One 3in square

Two 2½in squares cut in half diagonally

Two 3¼in squares cut in half diagonally

4 Take the larger triangles and sew them to the block in the same way as you did with the smaller triangles. Check the finished block is square, trimming if need be.

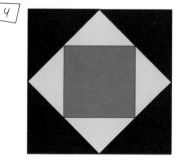

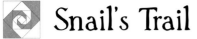

Snail's Trail

The instructions and diagrams here show this block with two colors, a dark and a light, and the secret of achieving the spiral is through the careful placement of the colors. Starting the block with a 2in square in the center and adding five rounds will produce a block approximately 7½in square. Cutting a strip about 18in × 5in from each fabric will allow you to cut down to the squares required as you make the block. Use a ¼in seam allowance.

1 Cut a 2in square for the block center from light fabric. Cut a 1¾in square from light fabric and another from dark fabric. Cut these smaller squares along the diagonal to give 4 triangles for the first round. Using ¼in seams, sew the 2 dark triangles to either side of the central square. Note that the edges of the triangle will extend past the edges of the square. Press seams outwards.

2 Now sew the 2 light triangles to the other side of the square and press. Trim the unit square (2½in if using the measurements suggested).

3 Repeat steps 1 and 2, omitting the central square, but this time, cut 2in squares to cut into triangles. Follow the color placement shown. Press well and trim the unit square.

4 Repeat steps 1 and 2, again omitting the central square, but this time cut 2½in squares to cut into triangles. Follow the color placement shown. Press well and trim the unit square (4in). Repeat this process for further rounds to achieve the block size you require, increasing the size of the triangles accordingly and pressing well at each stage. Trim the final block square.

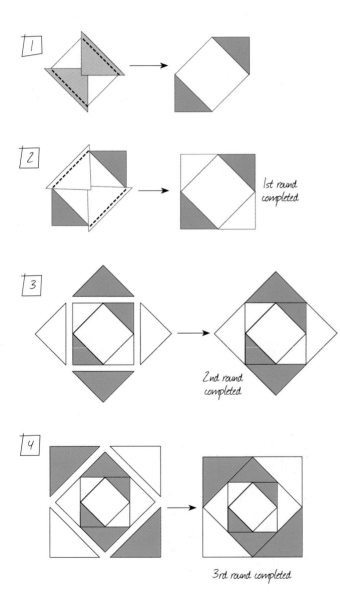

1st round completed

2nd round completed

3rd round completed

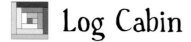 # Log Cabin

Log Cabin is one of the most popular patchwork blocks of all time and has many variations (see Courthouse Steps opposite). The block arrangement is one of strips, added in turn around a center square. The strips can be whatever width you choose and the block can have any number of "rounds." You will need one square for the center (usually a contrasting color) and a selection of strips in two contrasting colorways. Use a ¼in seam allowance.

1 First sort your strips into 2 piles according to colorway or tonal difference. Start by sewing strip 1, which is the same size as the center square, to the center square using a ¼in seam. Press the seam open. You can measure the length of strip required before sewing or sew a strip in place and trim it flush at the ends after sewing.

2 Sew strip 2 to the pieced unit, sewing along the long side, and press.

3 Now add strip 3 in the same way. This strip must be from the second colorway. Press the seam.

4 Now add strip 4 and continue adding strips in rounds like this following the numbers as shown until the block is the required size.

5 Press the block and trim it square.

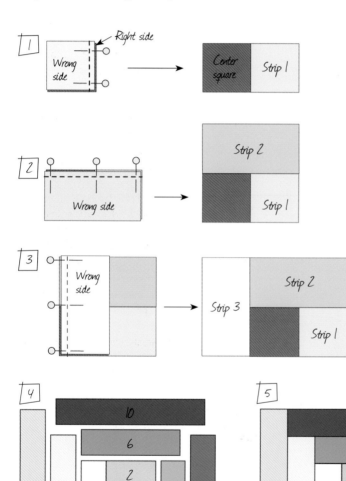

Courthouse Steps

This block is a variation of the Log Cabin block (see opposite) and is similarly versatile. The block arrangement is still one of strips added around a center square but this time alternating on either side of the square. You will need one square for the center (usually a contrasting color) and a selection of strips in two different colorways. The sizes of the rectangular strips all correlate to the chosen size of your center square. Use a ¼in seam allowance.

1 Cut appropriately sized strips from your chosen fabrics, remembering to add ¼in seam allowance all around. Sort the strips into 2 piles according to color or tone. Start by sewing strip 1 to the center square using a ¼in seam (the central square and strip 1 must be of different colorways). Press the seam open.

2 Sew a second strip 1 to the opposite side of the pieced unit.

3 Sew a strip 2 to the pieced unit—this strip must be from the other colorway. Sew it in place along the long side and press. Sew a second strip 2 to the opposite side of the pieced unit.

4 Now add a strip 3, changing the colorway back to the same as strip 1. Press the seam. Sew a second strip 3 to the opposite side of the pieced unit. Continue adding strips in this way, following the numbers as shown and alternating the colorways until the block is the required size.

5 Press the block and trim it square.

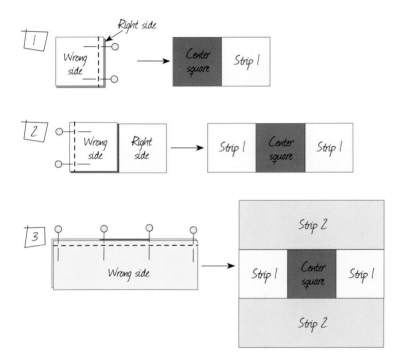

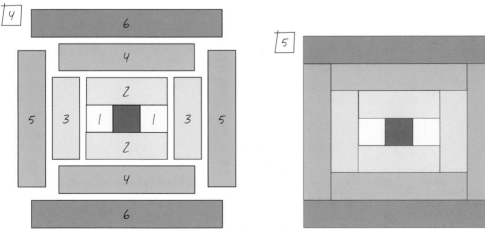

Boxed Square

When pieced from fresh, modern fabrics, this block can make a great contemporary quilt. You can also use up multicolored fabrics from your stash for a more scrappy look. To make one block you will need two small squares in one color, one square in a contrast color, and two rectangles. The rectangles need to be the same length as three squares sewn together. Use a ¼in seam allowance.

1 Sew together the 3 squares with the contrast square in the middle. Press the seams toward the darker square.

2 Now add the 2 rectangles, 1 on either side of the center row, arranged as shown.

3 Sew each rectangle to the central row of squares and press the seams toward the rectangles to finish block.

4 The Boxed Square block can be laid out in rows, perhaps with blocks with alternating colorways (4.1). Alternatively, you could rotate alternate blocks, which gives you fewer seams to align (4.2).

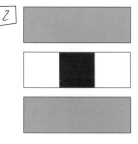

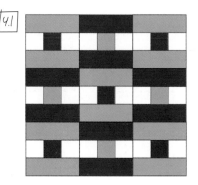

Basket Weave

This block couldn't be simpler to make and is a great one for creating a quick scrap quilt from lots of mixed fabrics from your stash. To make one block you will need one small square, one large square (twice the size of small square), and two rectangles. This is a block that can be made quickly with strip-piecing. Use a ¼in seam allowance.

1 Lay the blocks out as shown.

2 Sew together a rectangle and the large square. Press the seam toward the darker fabric. Sew together a rectangle and the small square. Press the seam toward the darker fabric.

3 Sew the 2 parts of the block together and press the seam.

4 This is a fun block to play around with—try a simple repeat with a limited palette (4.1), or go for multicolored scraps (4.2), or try rotating alternate blocks for a different look (4.3).

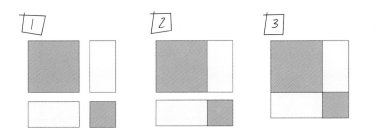

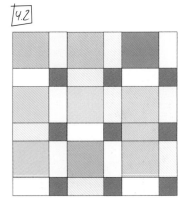

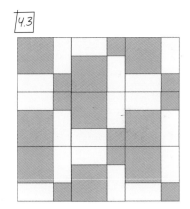

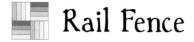 # Rail Fence

Blocks made of strips are best pieced with a method called strip-piecing. To make a Rail Fence block you will need four long strips in one colorway and another four strips in a second colorway. Grading the colors often works well. Use a ¼in seam allowance.

1 Using a rotary cutter, cut your strips to the width required across the straight grain of the fabric, to avoid too many stretchy bias edges.

2 Starting with the first set of 4 strips, pin 2 strips right sides together and sew together using a ¼in seam. Press each pair as you sew them. Repeat with the other pair and then sew the pairs together. Repeat this process with the second set of strips in the other colorway.

3 Measure the height of your strip-pieced unit and use this measurement to cut each strip-pieced unit into square segments.

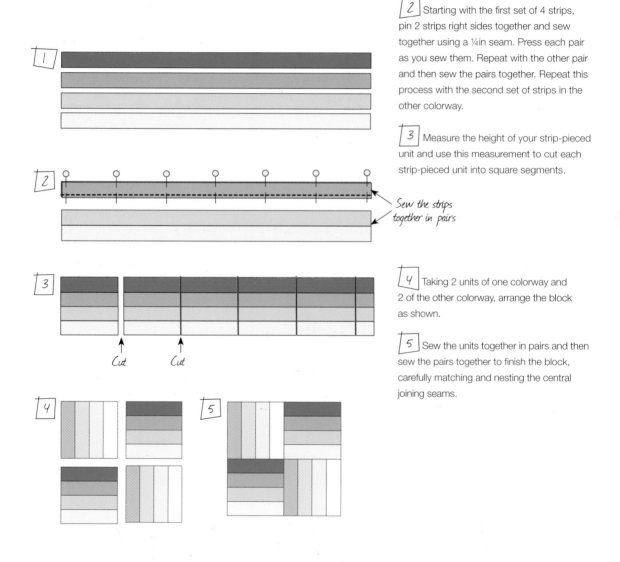

Sew the strips together in pairs

Cut   Cut

4 Taking 2 units of one colorway and 2 of the other colorway, arrange the block as shown.

5 Sew the units together in pairs and then sew the pairs together to finish the block, carefully matching and nesting the central joining seams.

Streak o' Lightning

This block is made from paired rectangles. The color placement is important in order to create the zigzag lightning effect. For the design shown you will need eight rectangles in a light color, eight in a medium color and 16 in a dark color. For a large area of this design it is quicker to use strip-piecing (see the Four-Patch block on page 164). Streak o' Lightning can also be constructed from Half-Square Triangles (see below). Use a ¼in seam allowance.

| 1 | The block is made up of squares made from just 2 paired rectangles in 2 different color combinations. Sew together a light rectangle and a dark rectangle. Press seams toward the darker fabric. Make 8. Sew together a dark rectangle and a medium rectangle. Press seams toward the darker fabric. Make 8.

| 2 | Lay the units out as shown, taking care to rotate alternate units and checking that you have the lightest streak correctly placed.

| 3 | Sew the units together in rows, matching seams neatly. Press the joining seams of the first and third rows in one direction and the seams of the second and fourth rows in the opposite direction.

| 4 | Sew the rows together, carefully lining up and nesting the seams. Press the finished block.

| 1 |

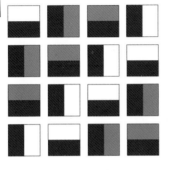

Make 8   Make 8

| 2 |

| 3 |

Streak o' Lightning with Half-Square Triangles

| 1 | A different version of this block can be created using 16 Half-Square Triangle units (see page 166). This alternate version still has the strong directional feel of the rectangular version, but with only 2 colors.

| 4 |

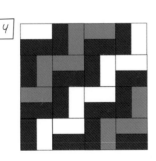

| 1 |

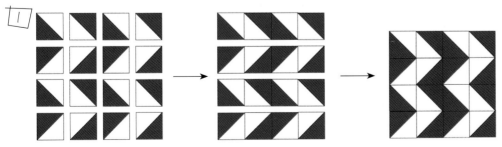

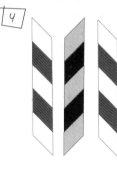

Chevron

A chevron pattern is very striking and the patchwork is easily created from strip-piecing, with segments cut at a 45-degree angle and rearranged in an alternating pattern. You could use tone or color, or both, to differentiate between the stripes, sticking with just two fabrics for a strong two-dimensional look, using multiple fabrics in two distinct tones or colors for a scrappy look, or, as here, choosing two fabrics plus a paler version of each to create a three-dimensional look. Use a ¼in seam allowance.

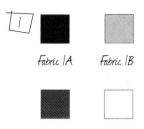

Fabric 1A   Fabric 1B

Fabric 2A   Fabric 2B

Fabric 1A
Fabric 1B

Fabric 2A
Fabric 2B

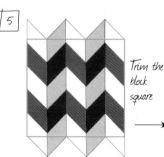

Trim the block square

1 To create the three-dimensional look you will need 2 sets of fabrics: a dark color and a paler version of it, and a light/medium color and a paler version of it.

2 Cut 2 long strips of fabric 1A and 3 long strips of fabric 1B, ensuring your strips are of equal width. Sew them together along the lengths with ¼in seams. Do the same with fabrics 2A and 2B. Press the strip units with seams on the darker unit upward, and seams on the lighter unit downward.

3 Using a quilter's ruler, cut the dark fabric unit into segments at a 45-degree angle. Cut the light fabric unit into segments at the opposite 45-degree angle.

4 Take 2 segments from the light colorway and 2 segments from the dark colorway and sew them together as shown, ensuring the seams nest snugly for a neat finish.

5 Trim the block square, removing the points at the top and bottom of the strips but allowing for a ¼in seam when joining blocks together.

Attic Windows

This block is made up of just three pieces but the choice of shading can create wonderful three-dimensional effects. It needs to be sewn with a set-in or Y seam. You will need three fabrics—one light, one medium, and one dark—in order to fulfill the visual potential. Use a ¼in seam allowance.

1 Cut your fabric pieces to the shapes required. The long pieces are cut as rectangles, with 1 corner trimmed off at 45 degrees.

2 On the wrong side of the fabric pieces, mark ¼in seam allowances all round, with a pencil dot at each corner, as shown by the red dots.

3 Pin piece A right sides together with square C, aligning the dots. Sew a straight seam from dot to dot as shown. Press the seam open.

4 Pin piece B right sides together with square C, aligning the dots. Sew from dot to dot as shown. Press the seam open.

5 Fold the unit diagonally, right sides together, so you have access to the final seam, joining A and B. Making sure that square C fabric is out of the way, pin and then sew from dot to dot as shown.

6 Press the finished block.

7 Joining blocks in rows creates a striking three-dimensional look.

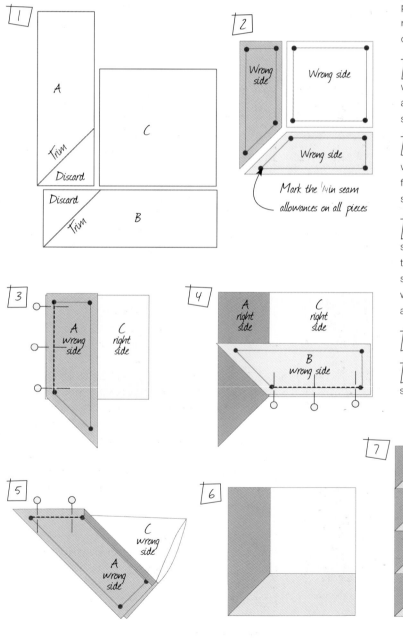

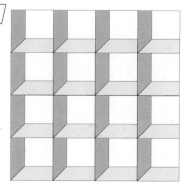

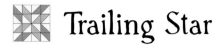 Trailing Star

Composed only of Half-Square Triangles, this block is deceptively simple but does rely on accurate piecing and neatly aligned seams. Specific placement of the 16 units creates the distinctive pattern. You need eight Half-Square Triangle units made up of a pale color and a dark color and eight Half-Square Triangle units made up of a pale color and a contrast color. (See page 166 for making Half-Square Triangles.) Use a ¼in seam allowance.

(See page 166 for making Half-Square Triangles.)

1 Make 8 Half-Square Triangle units from the pale color and dark color. Make 8 Half-Square Triangle units from the pale color and contrast color.

2 Lay out the units in the arrangement shown, taking care to place the Half-Square Triangle units in the correct orientations.

3 Sew the units together in rows, pressing the seams of the first and third rows in one direction and the seams of the second and fourth rows in the other direction.

4 Now sew the rows together, aligning and nesting the seams carefully. Press the finished block.

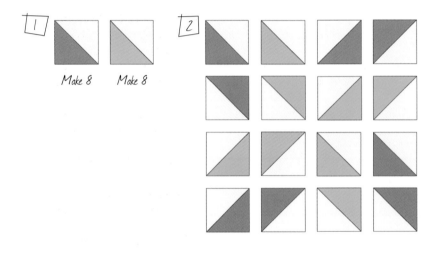

Make 8   Make 8

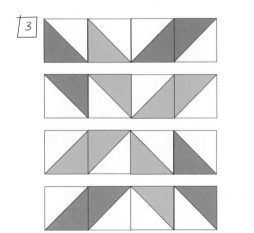

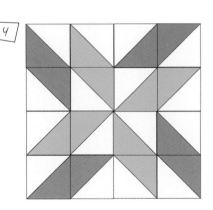

Le Moyne Star

This block has many names, including Eight-Point Star. It is made up of eight 45-degree diamonds, four right-angled triangles, and four squares but you could use Half-Square Triangle units (see page 166) instead of plain squares. The block shown uses three fabrics. Note that the diamond shapes can be elongated, if you wish, but as this will make them asymmetrical it is crucial to cut the shapes at opposite angles from the two fabric strips. Use a ¼in seam allowance.

1 Cut a long strip each of fabric 1 and fabric 2. Use a quilter's ruler to cut the fabric 1 strip into segments at a 45-degree angle. Cut the fabric 2 strip at the opposite 45-degree angle.

2 Take a diamond from each of the colors and sew them together. Repeat this with the other pairs.

3 From fabric 3, cut 2 squares in half diagonally to make 4 triangles. Using a set-in (Y) seam (as described in Attic Windows on page 191), sew a triangle to each pair of diamonds.

4 From fabric 3, cut 4 squares and sew 1 to each diamond/triangle unit.

5 Join the units together in pairs. Press all seams on one half to the right and all seams on the other half to the left to help with alignment in the next stage.

6 Sew the pairs together.

7 Press the finished block.

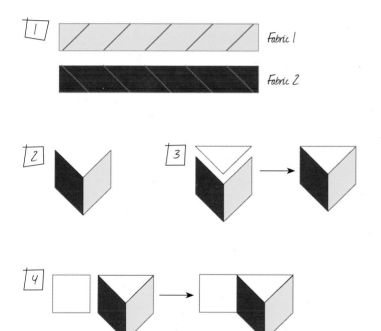

Fabric 1

Fabric 2

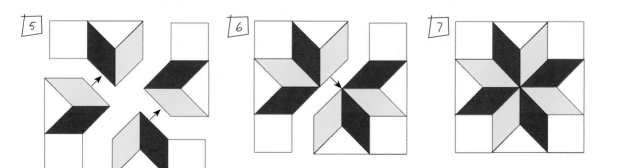

Windmill Star

This block is also known as Diamond Star. It is made up of four identical units, which create a square on point at the center of the block. Each unit is composed of four triangles—A, B, C, and D (C reversed). It is shown here pieced with templates but you could use foundation-piecing, specialist rulers, or even English paper-piecing. For the design shown you will need three different fabrics. Use a ¼in seam allowance.

Windmill Star templates—enlarge, add seam allowance, and cut from thin card.

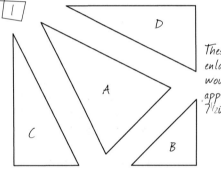

These templates enlarged 500% would make an approximately 7½in-square block

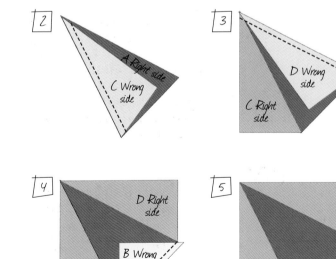

Make 4

1 Enlarge the templates to the desired size and add a ¼in seam allowance around each one. Cut out the template parts from thin card, on the outer line that has the seam allowance included. Cut your fabric pieces using the relevant templates. You will need 4 of each shape.

2 To make 1 unit, start by sewing fabric piece C to fabric piece A, placing the fabrics right sides together and aligning the pieces at the broad end of A. Press the seam to one side.

3 Sew the D fabric piece to the other side of A, right sides together, and press the seam.

4 Now sew fabric piece B to the A/C/D unit, right sides together, and press.

5 Trim the finished unit square. Make 3 more units like this.

6 Arrange the units as shown. Sew them together in pairs, taking care to align the seams. Press the seams open.

7 Now sew the pairs together.

8 Press the seams open and trim the block square.

Continued

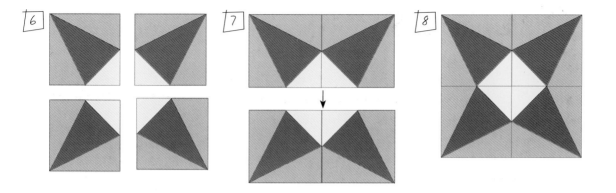

Windblown Star

This block is also called Balkan Puzzle and, because of the careful placement of the 16 Half-Square Triangle units, it has a nice rotational movement. You need eight Half-Square Triangle units made up of a pale color and a dark color and eight Half-Square Triangle units made up of a pale color and contrast color. (See page 166 for making Half-Square Triangles.) Use a ¼in seam allowance.

1 Make 8 Half-Square Triangle units from the pale color and dark color, and 8 Half-Square Triangle units from the pale color and contrast color.

2 Lay out the units in the arrangement shown, taking care to place the units in the correct orientations.

3 Sew the units together in rows, pressing the seams of the first and third rows in one direction and the seams of the second and fourth rows in the other direction.

4 Now sew the rows together, aligning and nesting the seams carefully, and press the finished block.

1

Make 8   Make 8

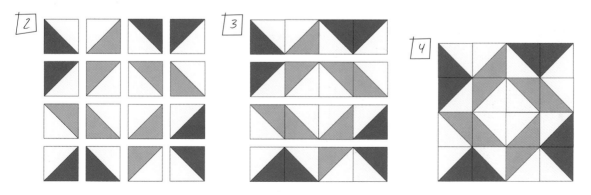

 # Kaleidoscope

This block looks very attractive when repeated across a quilt as the triangles form the illusion of curves. The block can be pieced using foundation-piecing or specialist rulers, or with templates, as described here. For the block shown you will need two fabrics: a dark color and a light color. Use a ¼in seam allowance.

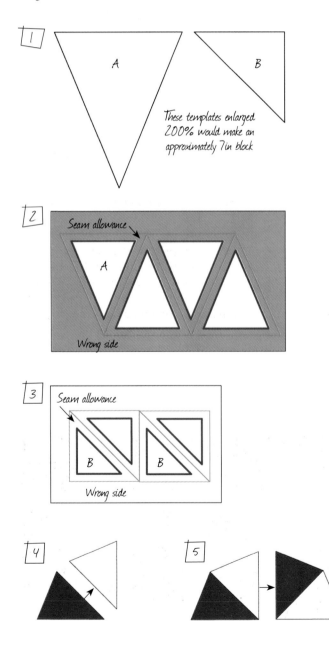

These templates enlarged 200% would make an approximately 7in block

1 Enlarge the templates to the size required and cut out the 2 parts (A and B) from thin card.

2 Place the A template on the wrong side of your dark fabric and draw around it with a pencil. Mark a ¼in seam allowance all round. Repeat, to mark 4 triangles in total. Then repeat to cut 4 more A triangles but using the light fabric.

3 Do the same with template B but on the light fabric only.

4 Sew the A triangles together in pairs of alternate colors, sewing from the broad end each time. Press seams open.

5 Sew two pairs together and trim dog ears. Repeat with the other 4 A triangles.

6 Sew the two halves together. Press seams open.

7 Sew the small B triangles at the top of each dark A triangle to form the corners of the block. When pinning in place, the small triangle should project out ¼in at either end.

8 Press seams outward.

9 If making a quilt from the same block, alternating the block colors will create an interesting effect.

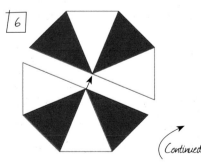

Continued

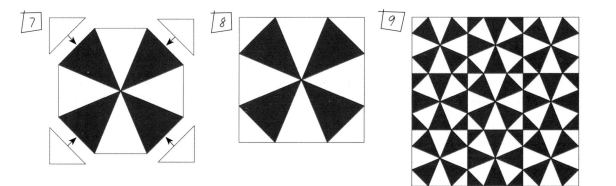

Ohio Star

There are hundreds of star blocks but this one remains a firm favorite. For the pattern shown you will need four dark squares, one square in a contrast color, and four Quarter-Square Triangles (see page 167) made up of a dark color, medium color, and light color. Use a ¼in seam allowance.

Make 4

1 | Begin by making 4 Quarter-Square Triangle units.

2 | Lay out the units in the arrangement shown, taking care to rotate the Quarter-Square Triangle units in the correct orientations.

3 | Sew the units together in rows, pressing the joining seams of the top and bottom rows in one direction and the joining seams of the middle row in the other direction.

4 | Now sew the rows together, aligning and nesting the seams carefully, and then press the finished block.

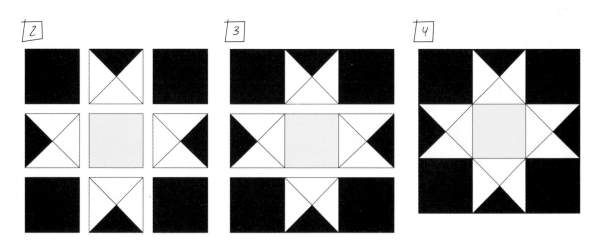

Six-Sided Star

There are many blocks made up of 60-degree diamonds and this is one of the simplest. It is an arrangement often made with paper-piecing, and is pieced in a similar way to Columbian Star (see page 200). It can also be machine-pieced using set-in (Y) seams, much like Le Moyne Star (see page 193). The block shown uses just two fabrics but more could be used. Use a ¼in seam allowance.

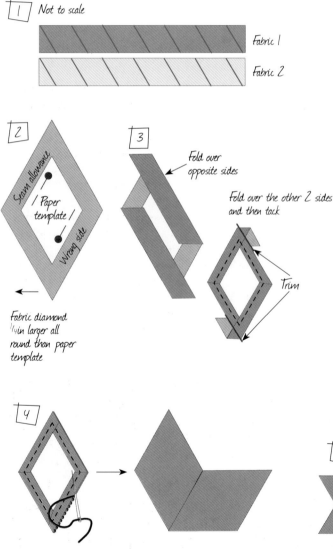

1 Not to scale

Fabric 1

Fabric 2

2

Seam allowance

Paper template

Wrong side

Fabric diamond ¼in larger all round than paper template

3

Fold over opposite sides

Fold over the other 2 sides and then tack

Trim

4

5

1 Create the diamonds using a long strip of fabric in each color and a quilter's ruler to cut the strips into segments at a 60-degree angle. Remember that all 4 sides of each diamond need to be the same length.

2 Make a diamond template from card that is ¼in smaller all round than your fabric diamonds—this is the master template. Use this template to cut 12 paper diamonds. Begin the paper-piecing by pinning a paper diamond template to the wrong side of a fabric shape.

3 Fold the seam allowance over the edges of the template, tacking in place through all layers. Trim off dog ears. Repeat with all fabric pieces in the colors required.

4 Working from the center of the design, sew the diamonds together in pairs with small whip stitches.

5 Now sew the pairs together.

6 Add the outer diamonds using the same whip stitch method as step 4. Press the work and remove the tacking and papers.

7 The shape of the block could be altered slightly at this stage if desired by trimming down the outer diamonds, but remember to allow for ¼in seam allowance all round if combining with further blocks.

Continued →

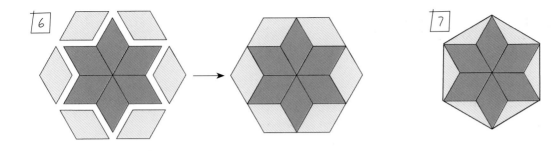

Friendship Star

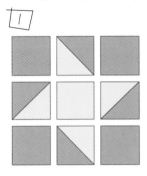

This old favorite is not only easy to piece but complements so many other Nine-Patch blocks. All you need are five squares (four in one colour, one in a second colour) and four Half-Square Triangle units. (See page 166 for making Half-Square Triangles.) Use a ¼in seam allowance.

 Lay out the squares and Half-Square Triangle units in the arrangement shown.

 Sew the units together in rows, pressing the seams of the top and bottom rows in one direction and the seams of the middle row in the other direction.

 Now sew the rows together, aligning and nesting the center seams carefully.

 There are many ways a Friendship Star can be combined with other blocks for lovely results. Here are some examples with Snowball (4.1) and Churn Dash (4.2). (See pages 180 and 178.)

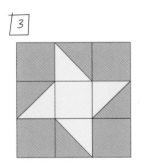

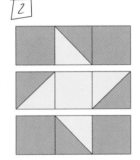

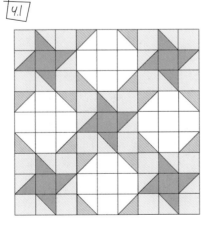

Columbian Star

This block is mainly made up of diamonds but has some triangles around the edges of the block to complete the overall hexagon shape. It is traditionally pieced using English paper-piecing, described here, but can also be machine-sewn using strip-piecing, with the block assembled in segments. For this you will not need the smaller diamond and triangle templates. Use a ¼in seam allowance.

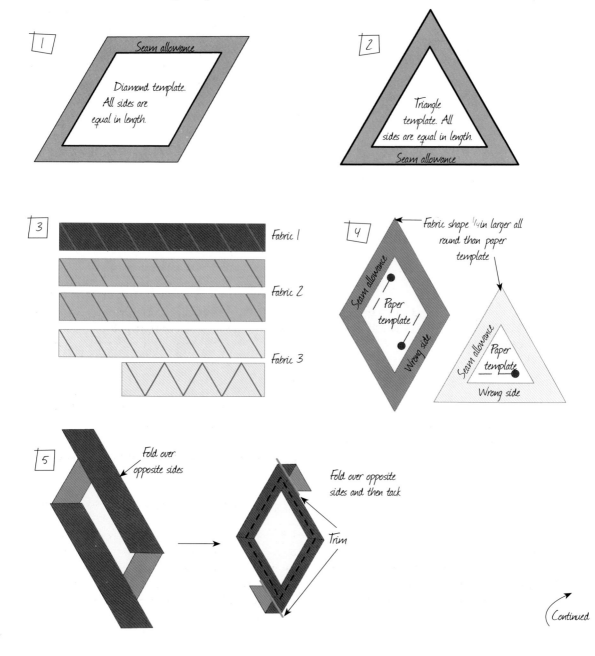

1 — Seam allowance. Diamond template. All sides are equal in length.

2 — Triangle template. All sides are equal in length. Seam allowance

3 — Fabric 1 / Fabric 2 / Fabric 3

4 — Fabric shape ¼in larger all round than paper template. Seam allowance / Paper template / Wrong side. Seam allowance / Paper template / Wrong side

5 — Fold over opposite sides. Fold over opposite sides and then tack. Trim

(Continued

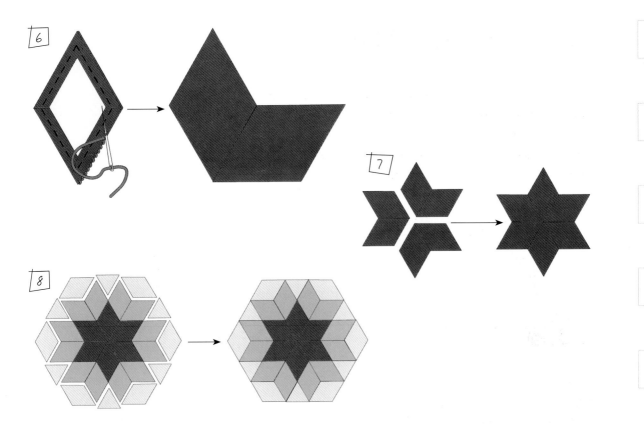

1. First make 2 diamond templates. The first should be the size of diamond you want to appear in your block, without seam allowance. It is shown here as the inner white diamond. Use this to create your second, larger diamond, which is simply the initial diamond plus ¼in seam allowance all round.

2. Make 2 triangle templates. The first should be exactly half of the smaller diamond, shown here as the inner white triangle, and is the triangle that will appear in your block without seam allowance. Use this to create a second larger triangle, which is the smaller triangle plus ¼in seam allowance all round.

3. Use the larger diamond template to cut 6 diamonds from the darkest fabric, 12 diamonds from the mid-tone fabric, and 6 diamonds from the palest fabric. Use the larger triangle to cut 6 triangles from the palest fabric. You should be able to line up the pieces to make efficient use of your fabric as shown in the diagrams.

4. Use the smaller diamond and triangle templates to create 24 paper diamonds and 6 paper triangles. Pin these to the center of each corresponding fabric piece cut in step 3, on the wrong side of the fabric.

5. Fold the seam allowance over the edges of the template, tacking in place through all layers. Trim off dog ears. Repeat with all the fabric pieces in the colors required.

6. Working with the darkest fabric, sew the diamonds together with small whip or overstitches, in pairs.

7. Sew the paired diamonds together to form the block center.

8. Continue working around the design, adding paired diamonds in the mid-tone fabric. Add the final, palest round, sewing triangles and single diamonds where shown. Press the work and remove the tacking and papers. The block can now be appliquéd to a background or further piecing can be added.

 # Triangle Hexagon

There are many blocks that use equilateral triangles (60-degree triangles). The block shown is a small one but the method described can be applied to sewing long rows of triangles and then joining them together. Your quilter's ruler should have a 60-degree marked line that will assist you. Specialist rulers can also be used. You will need six equilateral triangles for the block shown. Use a ¼in seam allowance.

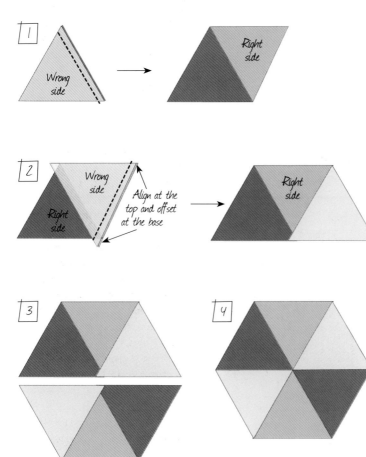

1 | Sew the first 2 triangles together, placing them right sides together and sewing from end to end in the normal way. Press the seam to one side.

2 | Place the third triangle right sides together with the second triangle, aligned at the top but offset at the base. Sew the seam and press to one side. (If you wish to make a long row of triangles, then the next triangle sewn on would be aligned with the base and offset at the top. Alternate this offsetting from top to bottom all along a row.)

3 | Repeat steps 1–2 to make another 3-triangle unit. Sew the 2 units together along the straight line.

4 | Press the finished block.

Tumbling Blocks

This block creates geometric patterns with a strongly three-dimensional appearance when grouped together. It is made up of three diamonds, sewn together with a set-in (Y) seam. You will need three different fabrics—a dark, a medium, and a light. It can also be sewn by hand in the same way as Grandmother's Flower Garden (see page 206). Use a ¼in seam allowance.

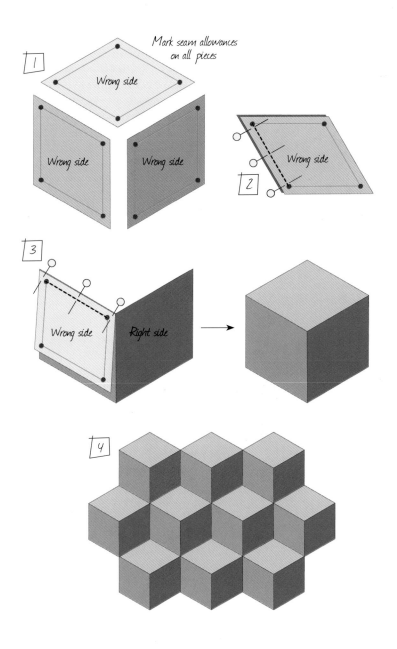

Mark seam allowances on all pieces

1. Cut your fabric pieces to the shapes required—1 diamond in a dark color, 1 in a medium, and 1 in a light. Diamonds can be cut from fabric strips, which are then subcut at the correct angle using the 60-degree lines on a quilter's ruler (see Six-Sided Star, page 198). Remember that each of the 4 sides of the diamond must be the same length. On the wrong side of the fabric pieces, mark ¼in seam allowances all round, with a pencil dot at each corner as shown by the red dots.

2. Pin 2 diamond shapes right sides together, aligning the dots, and sew from dot to dot as shown, backstitching a little at either end. Press the seam to one side.

3. Pin the third diamond right sides together with the edge of the left-hand sewn diamond, aligning the dots. Stitch from dot to dot as shown. With the needle down in the work, lift the presser foot, swivel the work slightly, reposition the seams, and then finish sewing the seam. (Alternatively, you can remove the work from the machine and reposition it.) Press the seam to one side. Press the finished block.

4. Use the same set-in seam technique to join the blocks together.

 Inner City

This interesting block is created from half hexagons. When units are tessellated, they create a three-dimensional design. It can be pieced by machine, beginning with strip-pieced units and then joining the individual hexagons with a set-in (Y) seam. You will need three different fabrics—a dark, a medium, and a light. The block can also be hand-pieced in the same way as Grandmother's Flower Garden (see page 206). Use a ¼in seam allowance.

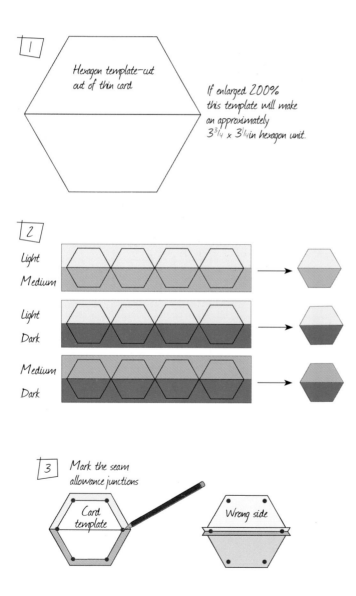

Machine-Sewing Technique

1 Prepare a hexagon template.

2 Cut fabric strips ½in wider than half of your hexagon template (if using the suggested size this will be 2½in) and long enough to fit 4 hexagons—2 light strips, 2 medium, and 2 dark. Using ¼in seams, sew them together into 3 units. Press seams open. Place the template on the right side of the light/medium fabric strip unit and draw around it 4 times. Do the same on the other strip units. Cut out the hexagons with a rotary cutter and ruler.

3 Mark the seam allowances on the wrong side of a fabric hexagon, with a dot at each corner, as shown by the red dots. You could cut the card template down by ¼in all round and use this to mark the dots. Do this on all of the hexagons.

4 Sew 2 hexagons together, right sides in, sewing from dot to dot as shown, backstitching a little at either end. Press the seam to one side.

5 Position the third hexagon and sew from dot to dot as shown. With the needle down in the work, lift the presser foot, swivel the work slightly, reposition the seams and dots, and then finish sewing from dot to dot. (Alternatively, remove the work from the machine and reposition.) Press the unit. Make 4 more units like this.

6 Join the units using the same set-in (Y) seam technique. When sewing multiple units together, sew the units vertically first and then sew the horizontal rows together. Sew the joined blocks to a background piece. If making a whole quilt, trim the edges of the patchwork to a square or rectangle.

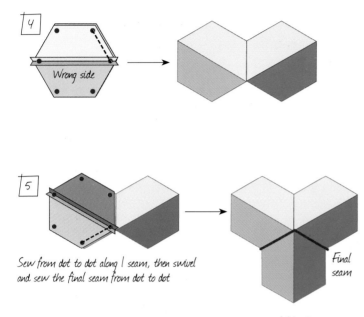

4

Wrong side

5

Sew from dot to dot along 1 seam, then swivel
and sew the final seam from dot to dot

Final
seam

Make 5

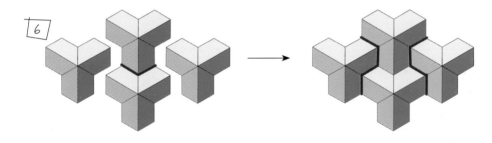

6

Hand-Sewing Technique

Follow steps 1–3 of the machine-
sewing technique to create the 2-color
fabric hexagons, and then refer to the
Grandmother's Flower Garden block
for the paper-piecing technique (see
page 206).

Grandmother's Flower Garden

This block is often created using English paper-piecing. The hexagon template, made from paper or card, can be any size you choose. The block can also be machine-sewn using set-in (Y) seams. Use a ¼in seam allowance.

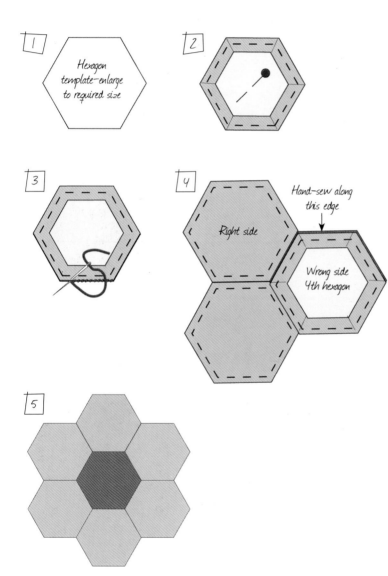

English Paper-Piecing Technique

1 Enlarge the template to the size you require. Use this master template to make 7 paper templates for the block shown. Make a second, larger master template by adding a ¼in seam allowance all round the original one. Use this template to cut out 7 fabric pieces in the colors of your choice.

2 Pin a paper template to a fabric shape and fold the seam allowance over the edges of the template, tacking in place through all layers. Repeat with all the fabric pieces.

3 Join the shapes into a flower by placing 2 fabric shapes right sides together, aligning the edges and using small whip stitches to sew them together through the folded fabric but not through the paper.

4 Place a third fabric shape right sides together with the second, and sew together. Continue adding hexagons around the central shape until the flower is finished.

5 Press firmly and remove the tacking and templates. The flower can now be appliquéd to a background fabric.

Machine-Sewing Technique

[1] Enlarge the template provided to the size you require. Use this master template to make a second template but this time add a ¼in seam allowance all round. Use the larger template to cut out 7 fabric pieces in the colors of your choice.

[2] Pin the smaller template in the center of a fabric shape and mark the intersections of the seam allowance all round with dots as shown. Repeat with all the fabric pieces.

[3] To join, sew 2 outer pieces together, right sides in, from dot to dot, backstitching a little at either end. Press seams to one side.

[4] Repeat with another 2 outer hexagons. Now sew 3 hexagons together, with the central one in the center.

[5] Sew the rows together. Begin at the points marked with an arrow.

[6] Sew along each seam from dot to dot as shown, backstitching a little at either end. With the needle down in the work, lift the presser foot, swivel the work slightly, reposition the seams, and then finish sewing the seam. (Alternatively, remove the work from the machine and reposition it.) Repeat all along. Press seams outward. Repeat for the other row. Appliqué the flower to a background.

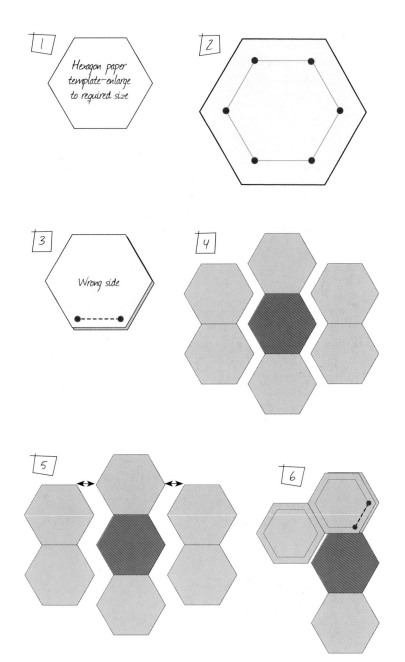

Hexagon paper template—enlarge to required size

Wrong side

Melon Patch

This block has a background of a Four-Patch block (see page 164), with the melon "seeds" sewn on top as appliqué. Traditionally, needle-turn appliqué is used but you could use fusible web instead. You will need two different fabrics for the Four-Patch block and the melon-seed appliqué.
A template is provided for the melon seeds—enlarge it to the size you require for your Four-Patch block. If using fusible web to fuse the melon seeds in place, a seam allowance is not required. Use a ¼in seam allowance.

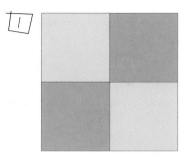

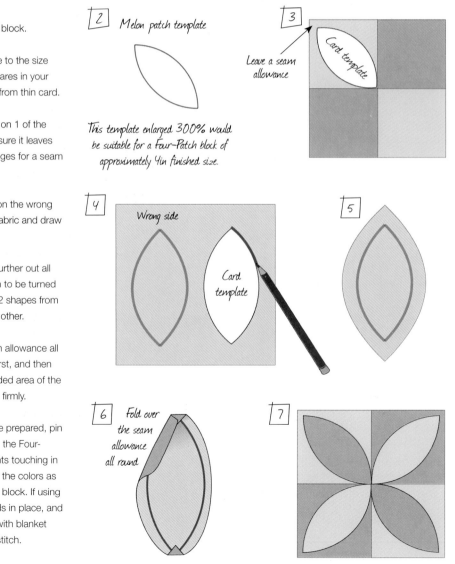

1 Make a Four-Patch block.

2 Enlarge the template to the size required to fit 1 of the squares in your Four Patch and cut it out from thin card.

3 Check the template on 1 of the Four Patch squares to ensure it leaves ¼in spare on the outer edges for a seam allowance.

4 Place the template on the wrong side of your melon-seed fabric and draw around it with a pencil.

5 Cut the shape ¼in further out all round, to allow for a seam to be turned under. Repeat this to cut 2 shapes from one fabric and 2 from the other.

6 Turn under the seam allowance all round—fold the tip over first, and then fold the sides over the folded area of the tip. Press the folded edge firmly.

7 When all 4 seeds are prepared, pin and sew them in place on the Four-Patch block, with the points touching in the center and alternating the colors as shown. Press the finished block. If using fusible web, fuse the seeds in place, and then edge the appliqués with blanket stitch or machine zigzag stitch.

2 Melon patch template

This template enlarged 300% would be suitable for a Four-Patch block of approximately 4in finished size.

4 Wrong side / Card template

5

6 Fold over the seam allowance all round

7

Grandmother's Fan

There are many fan designs but most are constructed in a similar way, with fan "sticks," a quarter circle in one corner, and a background piece. There are many ways to make the block, including machine-sewn piecing and appliqué. In this method two templates are used for the corner quadrant and the fan stick, and the design uses four different fabrics. Use a ¼in seam allowance.

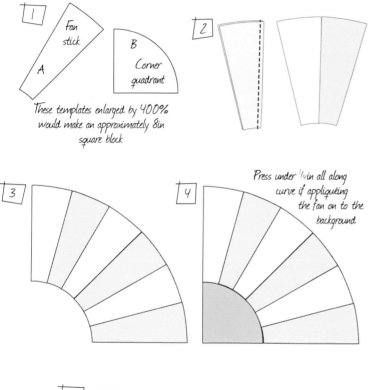

These templates enlarged by 400% would make an approximately 8in square block

Press under ¼in all along curve if appliquéing the fan on to the background

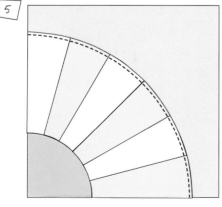

1 | Enlarge the templates to the size required and cut out the 2 parts (A and B) from thin card. Place the B template on the wrong side of your corner-quadrant fabric and draw around it with a pencil. Now mark a ¼in seam allowance all round. Place the A template on the wrong side of one of your fan-stick fabrics and draw around it with a pencil. Mark a ¼in seam allowance all round. Repeat to mark 3 sticks. Repeat on the other fan-stick fabric. Now cut out all 7 pieces of fabric on the outer lines.

2 | To piece the block begin by sewing the 6 fan sticks together with straight seams. Put 2 alternating fabric pieces right sides together and sew along the long edge.

3 | Add the next stick, and so on, until all 6 are sewn together. Press seams open to make sewing the curved seam easier.

4 | Sew the corner-quadrant piece to the pieced fan using a curved seam—see Drunkard's Path (page 210) step 3. Sew these pieces together from the multi-seamed side, as it will be easier to watch out for puckers. Use your fingers to keep the seams flat as you stitch, and stitch slowly and smoothly. Press the work carefully and then turn under a ¼in hem all along the outer curve of the fan.

5 | Attach the fan to the background square. You could do this with small slipstitches that don't show or with machine stitching ⅛in away from the edge. Alternatively, you could use fusible web between the layers and simply iron together. Press the work and trim the block square.

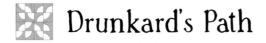

Drunkard's Path

This 16-patch block is an old favorite and there are many arrangements of it (see Love Ring opposite). Each unit has a single curved seam, which can be sewn by hand or machine. Templates are required for the two parts of the design. For the block shown you will need two different fabrics. Cutting the fabric pieces so that the curves are on the bias will help ease them together when being sewn. Use a ¼in seam allowance.

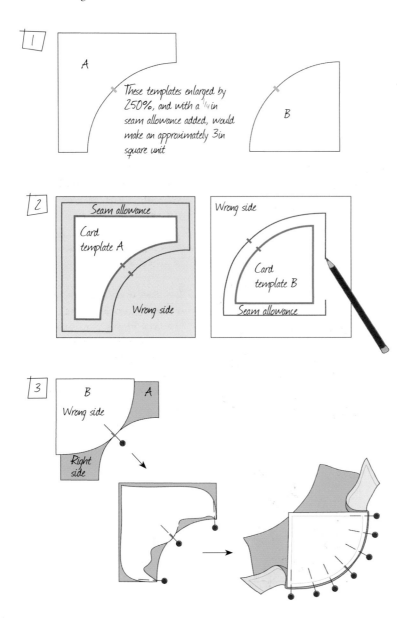

1 These templates enlarged by 250%, and with a ¼in seam allowance added, would make an approximately 3in square unit

2 Seam allowance
Card template A
Wrong side

Wrong side
Card template B
Seam allowance

3 B A
Wrong side
Right side

| 1 | Enlarge the templates to the size required and cut out the 2 parts (A and B) from thin card.

| 2 | Place the A template on to the wrong side of one of your fabrics and draw around it with a pencil. Now mark a ¼in seam allowance all round. Mark the center point of the curved edge of the template on the fabric. Do the same with template B but on your other fabric. Cut out the fabric pieces on the outer line.

| 3 | Place the pieces right sides together, aligning the center marks and pinning at this point. Now pin the 2 outer edges together. Pin the rest of the curves together, easing the fabrics to fit and pinning really well. Machine- or hand-stitch the pieces together along the ¼in seam line, stitching slowly. Clip into the seam allowance at intervals, but no more than ⅛in deep, to allow the seam to curve. Press the work from the wrong side toward the concave shape. Press again from the right side, using the tip of the iron to nudge the seam into a smooth curve. Trim the unit if necessary, to ensure it is square.

| 4 | Make 15 more units like this. Arrange the units into the layout shown.

| 5 | Sew the units together in rows and press. Ensure you alternate the direction in which you press so that the joining seams nest.

| 6 | Now sew the rows together and press to finish.

Continued

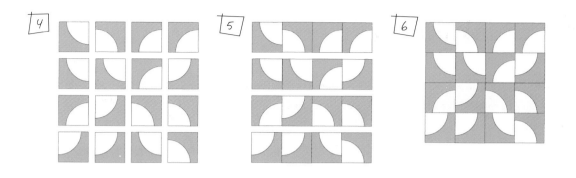

Love Ring

This is another arrangement of Drunkard's Path but here the colors are reversed for half of the units, so there are eight units with a light quarter circle and eight units with a dark quarter circle. The units are sewn in the same way as described on the page opposite. Use a ¼in seam allowance.

Make 8   Make 8

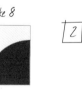

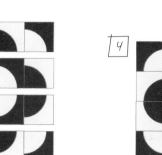

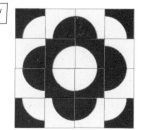

1 Follow steps 1–3 for Drunkard's Path (opposite) to make 16 units, but this time make 8 units with a light quarter circle and 8 units with a dark quarter circle.

2 Arrange the units into the layout shown.

3 Sew the units together in rows and press the joining seams of the first and third rows in one direction, the second and fourth rows in the opposite direction.

4 Now sew the rows together, aligning and nesting seams neatly, and press to finish.

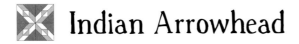

Indian Arrowhead

Color placement is crucial to achieve the right effect in this block. It is made up of four units, each with four elongated diamonds, two small triangles and two large triangles. It is best pieced using templates and a foundation-piecing technique or with templates alone, as described here. Alternatively, you could piece it more simply with Half-Square Triangle units (see page 166). Use a ¼in seam allowance.

1 Enlarge the templates and use them to cut your fabric pieces.

2 Begin by piecing an elongated diamond to each side of a small triangle.

3 The shapes need to be sewn together with offset seams in order for the edges to align correctly. Trim off dog ears as you go.

4 Now add the large triangle, taking care to preserve the triangle points. Make 2 units like this but reversing the colors in the 3-piece strip.

5 Sew the two halves of the unit together, matching the seams carefully. Press the seam open to reduce bulk. This is one quarter of the block. Check its measurement and trim it square.

6 Make another 3 units like this and lay out the block as shown. Sew 2 units together, matching seams carefully, and then join the 2 halves.

7 Check the measurements and trim the block square.

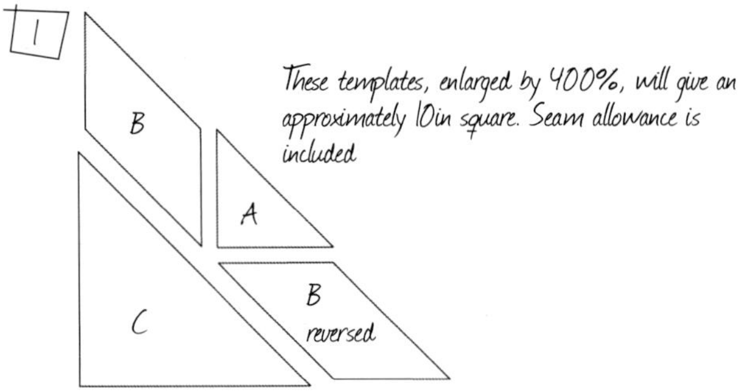
1
B
A
C
B
reversed
These templates, enlarged by 400%, will give an approximately 10in square. Seam allowance is included

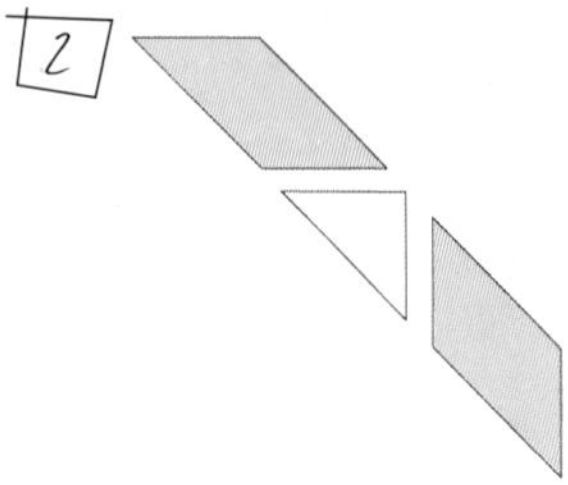
2

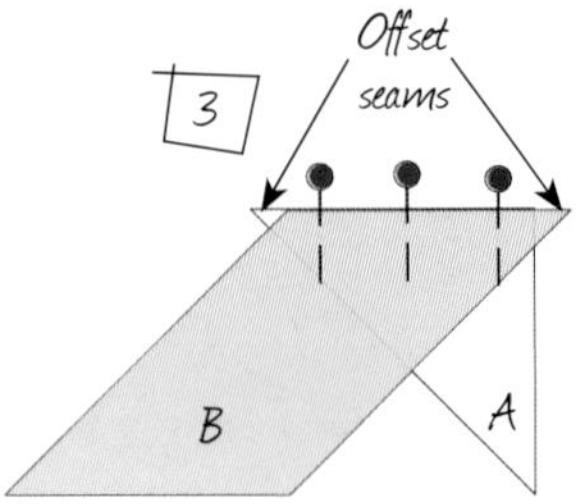
3
Offset seams
B
A

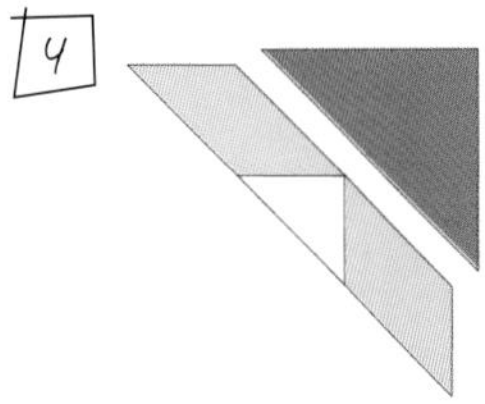
4

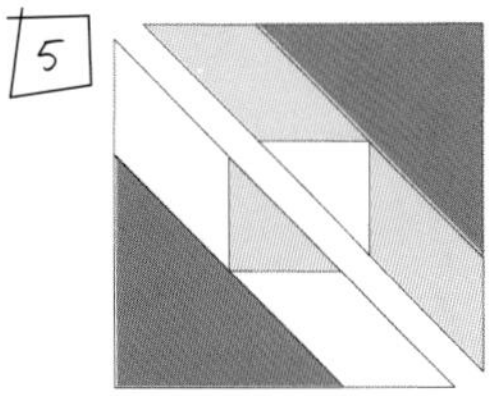
5

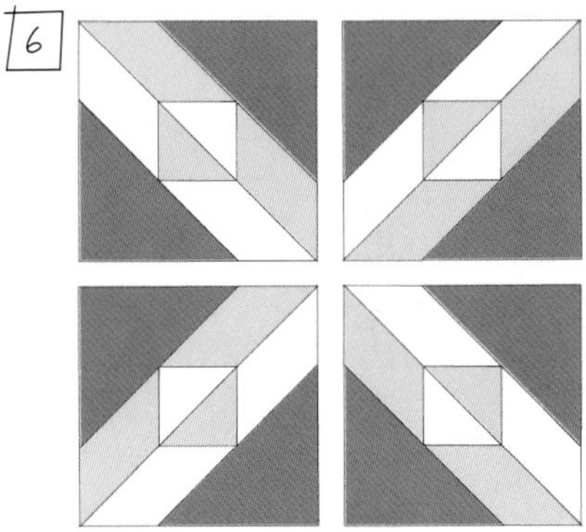
6

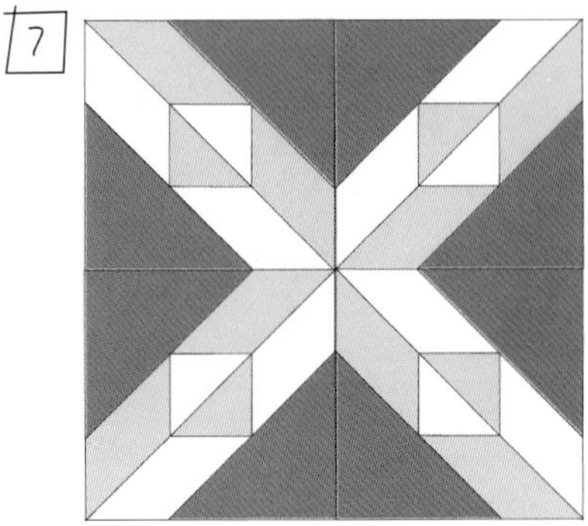
7

Crazy Patchwork

Crazy patchwork blocks can be created in many ways—as appliqué, as raw-edged patches, turned-edge patches, and with a machine stitch and flip technique (described here). Traditionally, the seams of Crazy Patchwork are decorated with embroidery stitches and trims. You will need a selection of fabric pieces and an assortment of braids, trims, and threads for embellishment. Use a ¼in seam allowance.

1 Start in the center of the block with a multisided, irregular-shaped piece of fabric. Place a strip of another fabric on top, right sides together, 1 outer edge aligned, and sew together with a ¼in seam. Flip the fabric strip over and press.

2 In the same way, add another strip of fabric, aligning its outer edge with the central patch and overlapping the first patch. Stitch in place. Flip the newly added patch over and press again. You could finger press for speed.

3 Continue adding patches in this way until your crazy patchwork block is the size you desire.

4 Press the finished block and use a rotary cutter and ruler to trim to a square. You could decorate the seams of the finished block using machine-embroidery stitches, hand-embroidery, thin ribbons, or trims and beads.

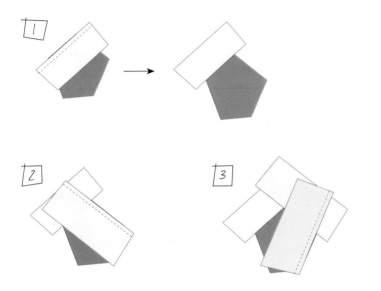

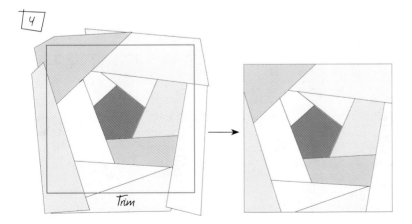

Trim

Assembling a Quilt

There are many different ways to assemble a quilt but the basic principles of layering backing fabric, some sort of soft "interior," and the quilt top, and then joining them together at intervals across the surface, remain the same. The instructions here cover the basics, but if you wish to take your construction techniques, quilting, and binding further, then there are many books, online resources, and classes available to help you.

Choosing Backing Fabric

The back of a quilt can be simple calico, a neutral cotton to tone with the quilt front, or a specific print to match the front of the quilt. The greatest design choice is with the normal 42–44in-wide fabric but this usually means joining fabric pieces. Extra-wide backing fabric is available as 60, 90, 108, and 116in widths, which is useful if you want to avoid seams in the backing. Prepare the backing fabric by trimming off the selvages and pressing.

Using 42in-wide Fabric

If your quilt measurement is 42in or less on one side, then you only need to buy one length of backing. For example, a quilt 36 × 50in would require 1½yd of 42in-wide fabric, which would give an extra few inches around all edges. If, however, the quilt were larger, proceed as follows.

1. For a quilt top size 60in wide × 80in long, cut 1 length of backing fabric 42in wide × 3½yd (126in) long.

2. Cut the yardage in half.

3. Rejoin the 2 pieces along the long sides to give a piece 84in long (minus a little for the seam)—this is enough for the length of the quilt. Press the seam open. Twice the width of the quilt is needed (120in), plus a few inches extra for the quilt sandwich, so 3½yd (126in) is enough.

1 Length of backing fabric 42in wide × 3½yd (126in) long

Quilt top 60in wide × 80in long

2 Cut backing fabric in half across width to give 2 pieces 42 × 63in

3 Join

Move 1 piece and sew the 2 pieces back together along long edges

Using 90in-wide Fabric

Using fabric 90in wide for a quilt 60 × 80in means that no joins are needed. The width of the fabric (90in) is enough for the length of the quilt (80in) so you only need to buy a 60in length, or 1¾yd, to allow a little extra for the quilt sandwich.

Making a Quilt Sandwich

A "quilt sandwich" is the term used to describe the three layers of a quilt—the quilt top, the batting, and the quilt backing. Once the three sections are layered, they can be temporarily fixed together in various ways to keep them stable while you do the permanent quilting. Basting is the traditional method but you could also use pins or safety pins, temporary spray adhesive, or plastic tacks. The backing fabric and batting need to be about 2–4in larger than the quilt top all round. Generally, unless you are using extra-wide backing fabric you will need to join fabric pieces to make the backing large enough (see page 214).

1 To make the quilt sandwich, press the backing piece, lay it right side down on a flat surface, and smooth it out. Depending on the size of your quilt, a dining table, bed with the soft bedding moved out of the way, or the floor can all work well.

2 Prepare the batting, shaking it out and making sure it is flat and large enough to fit the quilt plus a few inches extra. Lay it on top of the backing and smooth out any wrinkles.

3 Press the quilt top, ensuring that seams are lying flat, and lay it right side up on top of the batting. Make sure that the backing and batting are projecting out from the quilt top all round.

4 Use low-tack masking tape at regular points around the quilt sandwich to fix it to the surface it is laid out on.

5 Tack all 3 layers together with long lengths of basting thread, working from the center outward in a grid or radiating pattern. The lines of basting need to be about 4in apart to secure the layers firmly. Alternatively, pins or curved safety pins could be used to secure the layers, avoiding areas where you will be quilting.

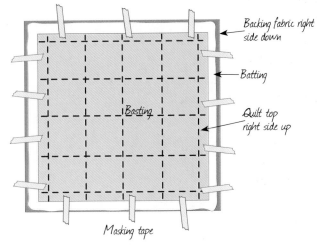

Backing fabric right side down

Batting

Quilt top right side up

Basting

Masking tape

Using a Spray Glue

The quilt sandwich can be fixed together using a temporary spray adhesive instead of basting or pins. Always read the manufacturer's instructions for the adhesive you choose to use. Long-term effects of glue on fabric are not known, so wash the finished quilt to remove any glue. Take care not to press the quilt top with too much heat as this could cause the glue to pucker the fabric.

1 Work in a well-ventilated area and protect surfaces with scrap paper or a sheet. Lay out the backing fabric and batting as in steps 1 and 2 of Making a Quilt Sandwich (above).

2 Turn back half of the batting, shake the adhesive well, and spray the turned-back batting lightly from a distance of about 10in. Fold the batting back over the backing fabric and smooth in place. Repeat with the other half of the batting.

3 Position the quilt top right side up on top of the batting and smooth in place. Turn back half of the quilt top and spray the batting half that is showing. Fold the quilt top back over the batting and smooth in place. Repeat with the other half of the quilt top.

Quilting

Once you have assembled and stabilized your quilt sandwich you are ready to permanently quilt the layers together. See Chapter 3, Adding Texture (pages 38–53), for more information about different quilting styles and methods. Marking a quilting design can take place before the quilt sandwich is assembled or afterward, depending on the complexity of the quilting design and personal preference. Marking methods are many and varied and include using chalk, pencil, and erasable pens.

Squaring Up Edges

After all quilting is finished the project can be prepared for binding by trimming and squaring up the edges. If there are any thread ends, deal with them by tying them off and burying them in the batting layer. If necessary, press the work gently to ensure it is smooth and crease-free using the steam setting on your iron.

1 Using a large cutting mat, rotary cutter, and large square quilter's ruler, carefully trim the batting and backing fabric even with the edges of the quilt top, making sure that the quilt is square by aligning the edge with the side and top of the ruler as shown. Move the quilt as necessary to continue trimming, aligning it with a previously cut edge to ensure all stays straight and square.

2 When the edges are neat, check the quilt's measurements by laying it out on a flat surface and measuring across its width in 3 places (top, center, and bottom) and along its length in 3 places. Make a note of these measurements. Ideally, the quilt should have the same measurement all across the width and the same measurement all along the length.

3 If one side is slightly longer than the other (less than ¾in) trim the long side slightly to even it up. Note that this is only possible with a plain-bordered quilt, not one with blocks right up to the edges where points or other parts of the block might be cut off.

4 If the quilt is more out of true, then blocking can help to straighten it. Lay the pressed quilt out flat right side up on a sheet on the floor, ideally on a carpet. Starting at one corner and using a rotary ruler, pull the quilt edges so they are square. Pin in place into the carpet or use a low-tack tape on a non-carpeted surface. Using 2 rulers will help ensure the corner is square. Move to the next corner and do the same. Secure the side between these 2 corners. Continue like this all round the quilt. Now measure and pencil a line on the quilt top all round the quilt, to the correct dimensions, which will indicate any areas that should be trimmed off later. To help the fabric set in this position, leave the quilt in place for at least a day. When the quilt is ready check the measurements one more time and then it can be trimmed along the marked line.

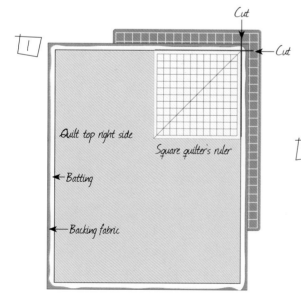

Cut

Cut

Quilt top right side

Square quilter's ruler

Batting

Backing fabric

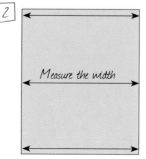

Measure the width

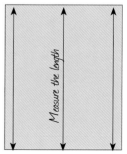

Measure the length

Making Binding

Making your own bias binding is a great way to finish off a quilt as the binding fabric can echo the fabric that has been used in the quilt. You can buy ready-made bias binding but the colors and patterns will be limited, and it's very easy to make your own. To work out how long a binding strip you will need, measure the quilt all round and then add at least 6in extra. Prepare binding at least this long. Strips are normally cut 2½in wide for a double-fold binding. Single-fold binding is usually around 1½in wide.

1 Press the fabric and cut sufficient strips in the width you require. If a single fabric is being used, aim for as few joins as possible. For straight binding, cut the fabric from selvage to selvage. For binding that has to go around curves, cut the fabric into strips at a 45-degree angle to the selvage, along the bias direction of the fabric, as shown.

2 Join the strips together into the length required. To do this, place 2 strips at right angles, as shown, and sew them together diagonally, which often looks neater that straight seams. Trim off excess fabric to within ¼in.

3 Once all seams have been sewn, press them open to keep the binding as flat as possible. Fold the binding in half along the length and press.

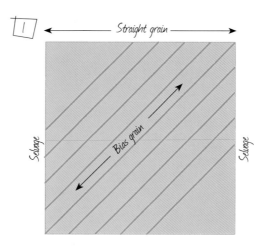

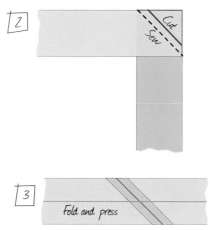

Binding

Binding can be single-fold (single thickness of fabric) or double-fold (two thicknesses), with double-fold being more durable but requiring more fabric. Binding can be attached in many different ways but the two most popular are straight corner binding and mitered corner binding.

Straight Corner Binding

This form of edging adds the binding in four separate strips. It can be sewn to show from the front or be pulled to the back more firmly so the edging is almost invisible from the front. The method described uses a single-fold binding with a starting width of 1½in.

1   Take two 1½in-wide strips of fabric, each exactly the length of the quilt, fold in 1 raw edge by ¼in and press. Pin the other raw edge of the strip to one side of the quilt, right sides together. Do the same on the other side and then machine-sew both strips in place using a ¼in seam.

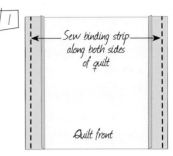

2   Turn the strips to the back of the quilt and hand-stitch them in place using small, neat slip stitches, and ensuring the pressed raw edge remains folded under.

3   For the top and bottom strips, measure the width of the quilt and add 2in to the overall measurement. Cut two 1½in-wide strips to this measurement. Turn over ¼in and press. Pin the strips to the top and bottom of the quilt as before, leaving 1in extra at either end. Machine-sew the strips in place as in step 1. Turn the extra 1in under at either end to neaten. Turn the strips over to the back of the quilt and hand-stitch in place as for step 2.

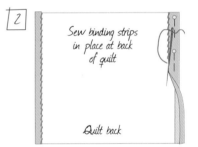

Mitered Corner Binding

This is probably the most popular way of finishing a quilt, creating neat 45-degree miters at each corner. The method described uses a double-fold binding, so you will need binding with a starting width of 2½in. Prepare sufficient binding for the project, plus at least 6in. Press the binding in half all along its length.

1 Sew the binding to the quilt by pinning the raw edge of the folded binding against the raw edge of the quilt—don't start at a corner. Using a ¼in seam, machine-sew the binding in place, starting at least 6in away from the end of the binding.

2 Take the quilt off the machine and rotate it as shown. Fold the binding up, creating a mitered corner.

3 Fold the binding back down, pinning it in place. Begin sewing the ¼in seam again, from the top to within ¼in of the next corner, and then repeat the folding process.

4 Leave about 8in of unsewn binding at the end. Trim off excess binding so the 2 ends overlap by about 2½in. Turn over a corner at the end of the binding to form a 45-degree edge in the double-thickness binding, and pin in place. Finish stitching the binding in place on the front of the quilt.

5 With the quilt front up, use a medium-hot iron to press the binding outwards all round. Turn the binding over to the back of the quilt, pinning it in place all round. Stitch in place using a matching sewing thread and tiny slip stitches, creating neat miters at each corner. The corner that you turned over at the end of the binding will create a 45-degree edge to cover the start of the binding at the back of the quilt. Press to finish.

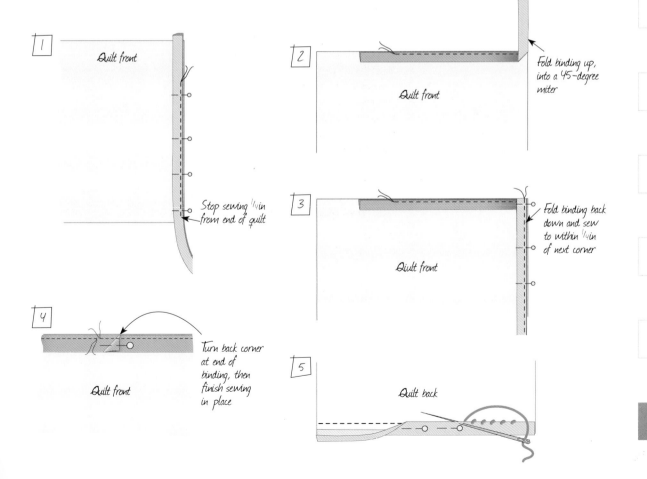

1 Quilt front
Stop sewing ¼in from end of quilt

2 Quilt front
Fold binding up, into a 45-degree miter

3 Qiult front
Fold binding back down and sew to within ¼in of next corner

4 Quilt front
Turn back corner at end of binding, then finish sewing in place

5 Quilt back

Resources

American Quilter's Society
www.americanquilter.com
Publisher of American Quilter and The Quilt Life.

Backstitch
www.backstitch.co.uk
Great range of Klona Cotton solids plus modern designer fabrics, with friendly, efficient online service.

Cotton Patch
www.cottonpatch.co.uk
Extensive range of fabric from generic blends to designer treats, with great notions range too, not to mention the excellent customer service.

Gone to Earth
www.gonetoearth.co.uk
Wide selection of modern fabrics as well as notions essentials.

Hawthorne Threads
www.hawthornethreads.com
One of the best websites for perusing fabrics—the range is gigantic and the site very easy to browse.

Keepsake Quilting
www.keepsakequilting.com
"America's Favorite Quilt Shop" has an amazing selection of quality cotton fabrics, patterns, books, supplies, and more.

Quilter's Haven
www.quilters-haven.co.uk
Well worth a visit if you find yourself in Suffolk, UK, but their online store is jam-packed with all kinds of fabrics in every theme you can imagine.

Stitch Craft Create
www.stitchcraftcreate.co.uk
Superb range of Freespirit Designer Solids, Tilda, and many more designer fabrics.

Books

The Quilting Bible (CPi, 2010)
The one reference every quilter needs. Its 352 pages and 1,000 photographs cover every aspect of machine-quilting.

Quilting 101 (CPi, 2011)
Written with the absolute beginner in mind, this book teaches all the basics for machine-quilting with step-by-step instructions and photographs.

The Quilt Block Book, Nancy Wick (CPi, 2013)
Teaches you three basic block construction methods to get you started in the world of quilt blocks.

Quilters, Their Quilts, Their Studios, Their Stories, Jo Packham (Quarry Books, 2013)
Connects you with 30 of the top quilters in the industry, so you can learn the craft from the best.

Index

Acknowledgments

Huge thanks to James Evans at Quid for commissioning me to write this book, and giving me the freedom to take the idea and run with it. Thanks to Lucy York for managing the book so efficiently through the production process, to Ali Walper for the lovely page design, to Dominic Harris for the beautiful photographs of both block samples and finished quilts, and the wider book production team for all their hard work.

To Linda Clements I owe a great debt of thanks for preparing the text and diagrams for Chapter 10: Her many years' quilt-making experience and depth of technical knowledge far surpass my own. Thanks also for coming to my aid at the eleventh hour and sewing the block samples for Chapter 9.

Thanks to Kate Haxell (www.katehmakes.blogspot.co.uk) for moral support throughout writing and sewing for the book, and for her impeccable quilting and binding on the Vintage Embroidery, Pretty Pastel, and Tumbling Blocks quilts. Similarly, a big thank you to Elizabeth Healey (www.elizabethsquarters.blogspot.co.uk) who made the Nine-Patch Cubed and the Big Chevrons quilts so beautifully, and to Jen Veall for spending three solid days cutting fabrics for quilts and block samples with the utmost precision.

Last but by no means least, thanks to my family: My husband Anthony and son Miles for entertaining each other when I was ensconced in my office sewing and writing, to my late mother Janet Lord for teaching me to use a sewing machine and encouraging me to "have a go" at just about anything, to my mother-in-law Christine Steward for her wonderful vintage fabrics, many of which feature in the book, and to our little cat Arthur, who modelled surprisingly patiently with the Swimming Pool quilt.